Field Guide to
CANDY

How to Identify and Make Virtually Every Candy Imaginable

By Anita Chu
Photography by Tucker + Hossler

QUIRK BOOKS
PHILADELPHIA

Library of Congress Cataloging in Publication Number: 2009924377

ISBN: 978-1-59474-419-8

Printed in Singapore

Typeset in Adobe Garamond, Franklin Gothic, and Impact

Designed by Jenny Kraemer
Photography by Tucker + Hossler
Production management by John J. McGurk

Distributed in North America by Chronicle Books
680 Second Street
San Francisco, CA 94107

10 9 8 7 6 5 4 3 2 1

Quirk Books
215 Church Street
Philadelphia, PA 19106
www.irreference.com
www.quirkbooks.com

Contents

SUGARY SWEET

CREAMY, STICKY, CHEWY

INTRODUCTION

Say the word *candy* and visions of brilliantly-colored gumdrops, soft chewy caramels, foil-wrapped chocolate bars, and rainbow-striped peppermint sticks come to mind. It is a part of many holiday celebrations, a treat for children, or a quick sugar fix. Indulging in a favorite candy bar or piece of fudge is one of life's finest pleasures.

The first candy was made when the ancient Egyptians coated fruits in honey to preserve them. Arabs turned the cultivation and refining of sugarcane grass into a booming industry in the 8th century, popularizing sweets in the Middle East and southern Europe. The word *candy* comes from the Arabic word *qandi* meaning "sugar."

In North America *candy* usually refers to highly sweet, vividly colored tidbits such as gummy bears, candy corn, and marshmallows. In the United Kingdom candies are called *sweets*; the British are famous for their many boiled sweets and chewy toffees. In France and other parts of western and southern Europe, the word *bonbon* refers to candies from chocolate truffles to candied fruit to marzipan. The term *confectionery* refers to sweet, sugary candies and pastries. But candy rarely contains flour or is baked in the oven like pastries and cakes. You shouldn't need utensils to eat candy—just pop it in your mouth.

There are several categories: **chocolates**, such as truffles, bars, and barks; **fruits and jellies**, such as candy apples and pâte de fruit; **sugary sweet** candies, such as lollipops and peppermints; **creamy, sticky, chewy** candies, such as fudge, divinity, fondant, and nougat; and **nutty** candies, such as peanut brittle, turtles, and marzipan. Additionally, popular **fun and simple classics**—from chocolate-dipped pretzels to kettle corn—are ideal for making with children or whipping up a quick treat.

This book will help you identify many of the most popular homemade candies around the world, discover what makes each one special, and re-create them in your home kitchen. You will also learn about some of the basic tools and techniques to make professional-looking candies, as well as simple ways to vary candy recipes to increase your candy repertoire. With this guide, homemade candies are just minutes away.

NOTES ON CANDY-MAKING TOOLS

Having the right tools to make candy will not only result in tastier candies but will also make the process more fun and enjoyable.

Baking pans. Although candy does not usually require baking, sturdy pans are essential: They hold liquid candy mixtures such as caramels or truffle ganache while they set. Baking pans should be at least 2 inches deep and made of glass, pyrex, or metal—preferably aluminum.

Baking sheets, also known as *cookie sheets*, are ideal surfaces for lining up individual candies to cool or set up. Choose heavy, solid sheets; thick sheets of shiny aluminum are best. Jelly roll pans, also known as *sheet pans*, are rimmed on all four sides. Rimmed pans are very useful for candies that require you to pour a large amount of hot sugar or chocolate, such as taffy, brittle, or barks.

Candy and chocolate molds. Truffles, chocolate bunnies, lollipops, and other molded candies are formed with candy molds made of plastic, rubber, or stainless steel. Although most hard candy molds can be used for chocolate candies, the reverse is not true. Not all molds are made to withstand the extremely hot sugar syrups used for hard candies, which require a maximum temperature of 375°F.

Candy thermometer. You'll need a thermometer that goes from 80°F to 400°F and has temperatures marked in increments of 5 for accuracy. Many thermometers have convenient markings for the different stages of cooking sugar.

Chocolate dipping tools. These small, flat, long-pronged forks or spirals are used to quickly dip candy centers into tempered chocolate without losing them. A regular fork or toothpick can be used instead.

Cooking spray greases baking sheets and baking pans for easy removal of candies. Use a flavorless vegetable oil–based spray to avoid adding unwanted flavors.

Food processor. This is helpful when grinding nuts and combining ingredients.

Gloves. Thin latex gloves protect your hands when manipulating hot sugar for taffy or brittle. Use non-powdered gloves to prevent contaminating the candy. Thin cotton gloves prevent fingerprints and other smudges on the shiny finish of molded chocolates.

Knives. A small paring knife is best when working with fruit and other delicate ingredients. A 6- to 8-inch chef's knife helps when chopping nuts and chocolate, or cutting candies.

Marble slab. This provides a perfectly smooth surface for working with candy; it also cools hot sugar mixtures quickly. If you don't have one, use a baking sheet.

Measuring cups. A graduated set of durable stainless steel dry measuring cups is best. Use a liquid measuring cup made of heavy glass.

Measuring spoons. Stainless steel measuring spoons are long-lasting and precise. Narrow, long spoons fit easily into small spice jars.

Mixers. Most of the recipes in this book can be made with a hand mixer or a stand mixer, and some recipes can be made by hand.

Parchment paper. Parchment paper is an excellent alternative to greased baking sheets. It is coated with silicone so candies come right off the nonstick surface without the mess of cooking spray or butter. Parchment paper is sold in rolls and precut sheets.

Ruler. A 18-inch metal ruler comes in handy for measuring candies and cutting them evenly.

Spatulas. Rubber spatulas are good for mixing ingredients and scraping candy batter out of bowls. Wide metal spatulas are indispensible for removing candies from sheets. An offset spatula has a long, thin metal blade bent slightly below the angle; use it to smoothly spread liquid candies such as brittles and barks and level dry ingredients when measuring.

Silicone baking mats. Baking mats made of silicone are the ultimate in convenience; candies come right off, there's no need for butter or cooking spray, and the mats are reuseable. Clean them with soap and water.

Wax paper. Place wax paper between layers of candies in storage to prevent them from sticking. Use it to line baking sheets, but do not put it in the oven or under candies made of hot sugar syrups; high heat can melt the wax coating.

Wooden spoon. The humble wooden spoon is an indispensible part of the pastry kitchen. A long-handled wooden spoon can be used to combine candy ingredients by hand or stir melting chocolate on the stove.

NOTES ON CANDY-MAKING INGREDIENTS

Most of the candies in this book can be made without any special or expensive ingredients. It helps to have a little knowledge about the most common candy ingredients to ensure the best results.

Baking soda. Baking soda, or *sodium bicarbonate*, reacts with acidic ingredients (such as corn vinegar, lemon juice, or cream of tartar) to form carbon dioxide. When it is added to hard candies like brittles or toffees, the resulting bubbles of carbon dioxide create a light, crunchy texture.

Brown sugar is simply granulated sugar with molasses added. Dark brown sugar contains more molasses than light brown sugar and has a darker, stronger flavor. When measured, brown sugar should be lightly packed into the measuring cup.

Butter used for candy making must be fresh and unsalted: It should smell sweet and feel firm. Butter should be kept well wrapped in the refrigerator because it can easily pick up odors. Avoid margarine spreads or other synthetic butter substitutes.

Chocolate. Several kinds of chocolate can be used for candy making. If recipes simply call for chocolate, use pure chocolate—either dark or milk. Dark chocolate refers to sweetened and bittersweet chocolates with 65–70 percent cacao content. Milk chocolate has added milk solids that give it a lighter, sweeter flavor; it can have as low as 10 percent cacao content. Pure chocolate needs to be melted and tempered to achieve a hard, glossy finish when it sets. *Couverture* chocolates are professional-quality chocolates with a high percentage of cocoa butter, which helps them melt smoothly and temper easily. However, couverture chocolates tend to be more expensive than regular chocolates, and the candies in this book can be made without them. Do not substitute chocolate candy bars or chocolate chips in recipes because they melt differently. *See also* Notes on Working with Chocolate.

Compound coating chocolate. Also called *confectionery coating, summer coating,* or *chocolate bark coating,* these products can be melted and used like pure chocolate, but they do not require tempering. They are formulated with added vegetable fats and oils that allow them to set up quickly with a smooth, shiny finish.

Confectioners' sugar. This is granulated sugar combined with cornstarch and ground to ten times the fineness of standard granulated sugar. It is also called *powdered sugar, confectionary sugar,* or *10X sugar.* Confectioners' sugar tends to clump; sift for best results.

Corn syrup. Corn syrup prevents cooking sugar from crystallizing. Light corn syrup works best since it does not color or flavor the candy. British *golden syrup* is made from cane sugar instead of corn.

Cream. *Whipping cream* or *whipped cream* is made with varying percentages of butterfat. Use a whipping cream with at least 36 percent butterfat; in North America this is usually called *heavy cream*. In the United Kingdom, *double cream*—about 48 percent butterfat—is best.

Eggs. Large eggs are the standard size for baking and candy making. Store your eggs in the back of your refrigerator, where it is coldest. Although you should keep your eggs fresh, egg whites that have aged for a few days will attain the most volume when whipped. Eggs should be used at room temperature: If you've forgotten to take them out beforehand, warm them in a bowl of lukewarm water.

Food coloring. Food coloring comes in liquid or paste form. It is easiest to add liquid coloring to liquid candy mixtures and solid paste coloring to solid candy mixtures. Food coloring paste is much more concentrated than liquid food coloring: A small dab is usually sufficient to color an entire batch of candy.

Flavoring extracts and oils. Flavoring extracts and oils give candies a variety of flavors, such as lemon, peppermint, and almond. Flavoring oils are more concentrated and stronger than flavoring extracts; they are often preferred by professional candy makers.

Flour. Store all flour in a cool, dry place away from light and heat.

Milk. Whole milk is generally best for candy making. A lower fat content can affect the candy's flavor.

Nuts. With distinctive flavors and crunch, nuts play an integral role in many candies. Nuts can go rancid quickly, so take care to choose fresh nuts and store them properly. When sealed, nuts can keep in the refrigerator for a couple of months or in the freezer for up to one year.

Sugar. Granulated sugar is the most common sweetener for candies. Store it in a cool, dry place; if it has hardened into chunks, break them up before measuring. *See also* Notes on Working with Sugar, page 19.

Vanilla is one of the classic flavorings for candies. Be sure to use pure vanilla extract; imitation vanilla extract has a chemical flavor and is a poor substitute for the real thing.

White chocolate. White chocolate is made of cocoa butter, milk solids, sugar, and flavorings. It does not contain any cacao, so technically it is not chocolate. Some countries have regulations on what can be called "white chocolate." Good-quality white chocolate is made with a high percentage of cocoa butter instead of vegetable fats.

NOTES ON WORKING WITH CHOCOLATE

Melting chocolate. Chocolate is a surprisingly delicate ingredient. The best way to melt it is over the gentle, indirect heat of hot water on the stove. You can use a double boiler, which is meant specifically for this purpose, or simply a metal bowl placed over a pot of simmering water.

The water should simmer but not boil, and the bottom of the bowl holding the chocolate should not touch the water. Chop chocolate into small pieces so they will melt quickly and evenly. Gently stir with a rubber spatula to prevent burning. Remove the chocolate from heat when it looks almost fully melted; stirring will melt any small remaining bits.

Melting chocolate in the microwave. Put finely chopped chocolate in a heat-proof bowl. Microwave it on 50 percent of maximum power in 10-second increments, stirring thoroughly after each interval.

Prevent melting chocolate from seizing. If a few drops of liquid get into melting chocolate, the cocoa particles in the chocolate clump around the liquid, turning the mixture into a grainy, chunky mass. So make sure your tools are dry. One common source of moisture is steam from the simmering water, so use a bowl that fits tightly into your pot. Do not cover melting chocolate; condensation may form on the underside of the lid and drip into the chocolate.

Saving seized chocolate. You can rescue seized chocolate by adding more liquid: Add 1 tablespoon of vegetable shortening or warmed cream for every 6 ounces of chocolate, and stir over medium heat. It will slowly turn back to a smooth consistency. Seized chocolate that has been rescued can no longer be tempered, but you can still use it in recipes that call for melted chocolate, such as ganache fillings (page 33–38) or chocolate fondue (page 269).

Tempering chocolate. Tempered chocolate has a shiny, flawless appearance. It feels firm and breaks off with a snap when you bite into it and it melts smoothly in your mouth, allowing you to fully enjoy the flavor.

Slowly heating and cooling melted chocolate while stirring puts it into temper. If chocolate is not tempered properly, the cocoa butter crystallization is uncontrolled and uneven, which results in an unattractive chocolate that is dull or has white streaks running through it. Untempered chocolate may feel rough or tacky and have a cakey, almost chewy texture. And it is more susceptible to heat and humidity, melting more easily and spoiling more quickly. Some simple candy recipes do not require tempered chocolate. However, candies such as truffles, dipped chocolates, and chocolate bars require tempering to achieve their signature appearance, taste, and texture.

How To Temper Chocolate

1. **Finely chop 1 1/2 to 2 pounds of chocolate. Smaller amounts make it difficult to control the temperature changes.**

2. **Place two-thirds of the chocolate in a double boiler or metal bowl set over a saucepan of simmering water. Make sure the bottom of the bowl does not touch the water. Place a candy thermometer or digital thermometer in the chocolate and stir frequently with a rubber spatula.**

3. **Do not let the temperature of the chocolate exceed 120°F for dark chocolate or 105°F for milk or white chocolate. When the chocolate has fully melted, remove the bowl from heat. Wipe the bottom of the bowl to get rid of any condensation.**

4.   **Stir in the remaining third of the chocolate a little at a time. Let it melt before adding more.**

5.   **Let the chocolate cool to about 82°F. If it is warmer, keep stirring and let it cool some more. If it is cooler, begin reheating in the next step.**

6.   **Once the chocolate is 82°F, place it back over simmering water. For dark chocolate, reheat to 88°F to 91°F. For milk and white chocolate, reheat to 85°F to 87°F. Remove the bowl from heat once you have reached the right temperature.**

7.   **Spread a small spoonful of chocolate on a piece of wax paper. If it looks dull or streaky, re-temper the chocolate, starting with step 2. If it dries quickly with a glossy finish and no streaks, the chocolate is in temper.**

Keeping chocolate in temper. Once melted chocolate has been tempered, it must be used before it cools and sets. If it cools to about 84°F to 86°F and is still fairly liquid, it can be reheated to a liquid consistency. If it has completely cooled and solidified, it should be re-tempered. Heat it for 5 to 10 seconds at a time, stirring and checking the temperature before re-heating. For dark chocolate, reheat to 88°F to 91°F. For milk and white chocolate, reheat to 87°F to 88°F. If you keep your chocolate within these temperature ranges, it will stay in temper and be liquid enough to use.

Easy alternatives to tempering chocolate. Several products exist for those who do not want to temper chocolate. They are called *confection-ery coatings, coating chocolate, summer coating,* or *chocolate bark coatings*. They are usually made of vegetable fats that melt smoothly and set up quickly to a finish that is very similar to tempered chocolate. They may not contain actual chocolate. Nothing can perfectly duplicate the taste and mouth-feel of tempered chocolate, but quality coatings can be good substitutes. They can be cooled and reheated quickly, and as often as necessary.

NOTES ON WORKING WITH SUGAR

Many candies are made by boiling sugar and water at high temperatures to make sugar syrup. Sugar syrups heated to different temperature stages cool to different consistencies, making different types of candy. For example, soft, creamy fudge is cooked to a much lower temperature than hard, shiny lollipops.

There are two ways to determine the stage of sugar syrup: a candy thermometer or the cold water test. A candy thermometer is the most convenient, modern method for checking cooking sugar. The cold water test is the classic method for checking cooking sugar. It was devised by the English and French in the 17th century, before the general availability of home thermometers. Dropping a small amount of hot sugar syrup into a bowl of cold water halts the cooking and indicates the sugar stage. The names of the stages of boiling sugar are based on the forms they take in the cold water test.

Sugar Cooking Chart

Temperature	Sugar stage	Candy
223°F–234°F	**Thread:** The sugar drips from a spoon and stretches into thin threads in cold water.	
235°F–240°F	**Soft ball:** The sugar forms into a ball in cold water but loses its shape when taken out.	Fudge and fondant
245°F–250°F	**Firm ball:** The sugar forms into a ball in cold water and remains a ball when taken out, but it loses its shape when pressed.	Caramels
250°F–264°F	**Hard ball:** The sugar forms into a ball in cold water and remains a ball when take out. It keeps its shape when pressed but still feels sticky.	Nougat and marshmallows
270°F–290°F	**Soft crack:** The sugar forms into long threads in cold water. The threads are stretchy and slightly sticky when taken out.	Butterscotch
298°F–310°F	**Hard crack:** The sugar forms into long threads in cold water. The threads are brittle and snap easily when taken out.	Hard candies and brittle
320°F and above	**Caramel:** The sugar turns golden yellow. Nearly all the water has been boiled out of the syrup. If it continues cooking, it will burn and turn black.	

Cook sugar on a clear, dry day. Because sugar absorbs water, humidity can lengthen the cooking process or prevent the cooking sugar from reaching the right stage and setting up properly. If it's raining, turn on air-conditioning to make your kitchen as cool and dry as possible.

Cook sugar in a large, heavy-bottomed saucepan with at least a 3-quart capacity. Aluminum and copper saucepans are best because they conduct heat evenly. Copper saucepans should be unlined; some copper cookware is lined with tin or other materials that can melt under very high sugar-cooking temperatures. Many confectioners use a sugar pot, which is simply a large all-copper saucepan made for cooking sugar. Sugar pots and other copper cookware can be found at most cooking stores.

Watch for crystallization that can ruin sugar syrup. This happens when a stray sugar crystal or particle gets into sugar syrup. Agitating the syrup at the wrong time can cause crystallization. You will see crystals of sugar forming in the syrup, and the entire mixture may turn into a crackly, solid mass. Throw out the crystallized sugar mixture and start again with a clean saucepan.

Use ingredients that prevent crystallization. Helpful ingredients called *doctors* or *interfering agents* guard against crystallization: acids, such as cream of tartar or lemon juice; glucose, such as corn syrup; and fats, such as butter or cream.

Icon Key

TOOLS			
stand mixer	pastry bag	fridge	oven
stovetop heat	spoon	bowl	sharp knife
small cookie cutters	candy molds	pastry brush	whisk
baking sheet	baking pan	saucepan	kitchen shears
metal spatula	rubber spatula	candy thermometer	food processor

SERVING & STORAGE SUGGESTIONS			
spring	summer	fall	winter
airtight container	gift	candy wrappers	Halloween candy

MISCELLANEOUS			
photo	time	caution	no humidity
tempered chocolate	parchment or wax paper		

All Things Chocolate

1a–b.   **CHOCOLATE BARK**

General
Description: *Chocolate bark is the simplest of homemade candy bars,*
consisting of a slab of tempered chocolate studded with
toppings and broken into irregular pieces. It comes in
an astonishing variety of flavor combinations; dark
chocolate is most common, but white chocolate with
peppermint is an eye-catching seasonal favorite. It
does not require any molds or fancy finishing—just
a flat baking sheet and some creativity.

History: Chocolate bark was invented by chocolatiers to use
up leftover tempered chocolate when making truffles,
chocolate bunnies, orangettes, and other candies.

Serving
Suggestions: Any kind of tempered chocolate can be used.
Experiment with the toppings of your choice. Try
nuts, dried fruits, seeds, and even crushed candies:
pralines, **candied fruit**, or **chocolate-dipped pretzels**.

Candy-Making
Notes: Bark is an excellent way to use up tempered chocolate
left over after making other chocolates.

Recipes: ***Dark Chocolate and Nut Bark***

14 ounces bittersweet chocolate
1 cup almonds, toasted and chopped

³/₄ **cup dried cranberries**

1. **Line a baking sheet with parchment paper.**

2. **Melt and temper the chocolate (page 17).**

3. **Pour chocolate onto the baking sheet and spread it about ³/₈ inch thick.**

4. **Sprinkle almonds and cranberries over the chocolate. Press them lightly so they stick. Let the chocolate set, about 1 hour.**

5. **Break bark into small irregular pieces with your hands or a sharp chef's knife.**

Yield: About 24 pieces

Storage: Store in an airtight container in a cool, dry place for up to 1 week.

Peppermint Bark
This bark is a Christmastime classic, perfect for gift baskets.

14 ounces bittersweet chocolate
14 ounces white chocolate
¹/₂ cup peppermint candies, crushed

1. **Line a baking sheet with parchment paper.**

2. **Melt and temper the chocolate (page 17).**

3. **Pour chocolate onto the baking sheet and spread it to about $^1/_4$ inch thick. Let it set, about 30 minutes. Temper the white chocolate while it is hardening.**

4. **Pour the white chocolate over the bittersweet chocolate layer and spread it evenly.**

5. **Sprinkle crushed candy pieces over the white chocolate. Press them lightly so they stick. Let the white chocolate set, about 30 minutes.**

6. **Break bark into small, irregular pieces.**

Yield: About 24 pieces

Storage: Store in an airtight container in a cool, dry place for up to 1 week.

2a–b. 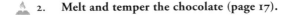 **CHOCOLATE BARS**

General
Description: *Charlie Bucket could afford only one candy a year, and he always chose a Willy Wonka chocolate bar.* Hershey's iconic rectangular bars of milk chocolate are the most famous, but now a variety of high-end chocolate

bars showcase the flavors of cacao beans from around the world. The higher the percentage of cacao bean content, the darker the chocolate bar.

History:

The Azetec ruler Montezuma served a spicy, bitter chocolate drink to Spanish conquistador Hernan Cortez in 1519. The Spanish took cacao beans to Europe, and decades later rich Europeans drank chocolate made of finely ground cacao beans mixed with cinnamon and vanilla or milk and sugar. In 1847, English confectioner Joseph Fry discovered how to recombine cocoa butter with cocoa powder to make a paste that could be molded and hardened to a solid: the first chocolate bars. These early chocolates weren't the smooth bars we know today until 1879, when Rudolphe Lindt of Switzerland invented the conching machine that works chocolate into a smooth consistency.

Serving Suggestions:

Making chocolate bars from beans is a labor-intensive process, but tempering and pouring your favorite chocolate into molds is easy. Homemade chocolate bars are a sweet gift year-round.

Candy-Making Notes:

Sprinkle in nuts, dried fruits, cocoa nibs, or other additions after step 4.

Recipe:

16 ounces bittersweet, semisweet, milk, or white chocolate

1. **Check that the mold is completely clean and dry.**

2. **Melt and temper the chocolate (page 17).**

3. **Carefully ladle tempered chocolate into the mold cavities, filling them to the top. Tap the mold lightly to eliminate air bubbles.**

4. **Using a spatula, scrape away any extra chocolate, leaving the tops clean and level.**

5. **Place mold in the refrigerator for 15 to 30 minutes.**

6. **Remove it from the refrigerator when the chocolate looks firm and is starting to shrink away from the sides of the mold. Flip it over onto a clean surface to unmold chocolate bars.**

Yield: About 5 chocolate bars

Storage: Wrap bars in foil or store them in an airtight container in a cool, dry place for up to 1 month.

Variation: ***Filled Chocolate Bars***
Many of the fillings in this book can be used to fill chocolate bars. Try mint ganache (page 48), caramel (page 47), or melted fondant (page 178).

1. **Ladle tempered chocolate into the mold cavities.**

2. **Invert the mold over the bowl containing the tempered chocolate, letting excess chocolate run out until just a thin layer of chocolate remains.**

3. **Refrigerate mold for 10 to 15 minutes.**

4. **When chocolate is firm, pour in the filling of your choice, to just below the top of the cavities. Refrigerate for another 15 minutes to let the filling set slightly.**

5. **Ladle tempered chocolate over the top of the mold. Using a spatula, scrape off the excess, leaving the tops completely clean and level. Refrigerate 20 minutes before unmolding the bars.**

Yield: About 10 filled chocolate bars

Storage: Store in an airtight container in a cool, dry place for up to 2 weeks.

3. ## CHOCOLATE NOUGATS

General Description: *Fluffy, chocolate-flavored nougat fills chocolates and candy bars in North America.* Nougat filling is much softer than European **nougat**. One of the most well-known nougat-filled candy bars is 3 Musketeers, which has a very fluffy, chocolate-flavored filling similar to this recipe.

History:
In the 1920s, the Pendergast Candy Company in Minneapolis reportedly put too many egg whites into one of their batches of dark, chewy, European-style **nougat**. The resulting airy concoction was used in their Fat Emma bar, and it proved so popular that it became known as "Minneapolis nougat." Frank Mars of Mars, Inc., created his own nougat-filled bar, the Milky Way. He turned Mars, Inc., into a candy powerhouse that went on to create other nougat-filled bars, such as Snickers, 3 Musketeers, and Mars Bars.

Serving Suggestions:
These chocolate nougats are a wonderful treat for kids on Halloween. Dipped in your favorite bittersweet chocolate and nestled in foil cups, they are elegant enough for dinner parties. Try adding toasted nuts on top of the nougat centers before dipping them in chocolate.

Candy-Making Notes:
Be sure to whip the mixture until it is stiff and thick so that the nougat will stay light and fluffy.

Recipe:
2 egg whites
2 cups sugar
1$^1/_3$ cups light corn syrup
$^1/_4$ teaspoon salt
1 teaspoon vanilla extract

¼ cup unsalted butter, room temperature
3 ounces semisweet chocolate, melted
⅓ cup cocoa powder, sifted
1 pound bittersweet or coating chocolate

1. Line an 8-by-8-inch baking pan with foil and grease well.

2. Whisk the egg whites in a stand mixer on high speed until soft peaks form.

3. In a saucepan, combine sugar, corn syrup, ½ cup water, and salt. Cook over medium heat until it reaches a boil. Continue cooking until the mixture reaches 270°F, soft crack stage.

4. While the mixer is running, slowly pour the hot sugar syrup into the egg whites. Continue to beat until the mixture is stiff and glossy, about 5 minutes.

5. Mix in the vanilla extract, butter, and melted chocolate.

6. Add cocoa powder and beat until combined.

7. Pour mixture onto the baking pan. Cover with plastic wrap and refrigerate overnight.

8. **Cut nougat into pieces with a well-oiled knife. Line a baking sheet with parchment or wax paper.**

9. **Melt and temper the chocolate (page 17).**

10. **Dip nougats in chocolate with a dipping fork, coating completely. Let set on baking sheet 1 hour.**

Yield: About 50 pieces

 Storage: Store in an airtight container in a cool, dry place for up to 1 week.

4a–c. **DIPPED CHOCOLATES**

General Description: *Although many candies are dipped in chocolate, in confectioner's terms a dipped chocolate is a small square of ganache or other solid filling hand-dipped in tempered chocolate.* It is similar to a **truffle**: both are made by enrobing ganache in tempered chocolate. The flat tops of these square chocolates are beautifully decorated with hand-applied color, glitter, or decorative patterns that are clues to the flavors inside.

History: Dipped chocolates originated in the fine chocolate shops of France. At first, their sleek, minimalist designs were a stark counterpoint to the fancifully formed and elaborately decorated **truffles** and **filled**

molded chocolates. But recently chocolatiers have begun decorating dipped chocolates in colorful and distinctive ways. One of the biggest innovations was transfer sheets, invented by chocolatier Jean-Pierre Wybauw in 1965. These thin sheets of acetate are coated with edible inks applied in a variety of designs—from swirls to dots to words—that can be pressed onto the tops of dipped chocolates.

Serving Suggestions:

Select toppings that match the flavor of the filling inside. Transfer sheets come in an array of colorful and eye-catching patterns to suit any occasion.

Candy-Making Notes:

Keeping the chocolate in temper—at the right consistency and temperature—will allow you to dip your chocolates quickly and consistently.

Recipes:

Vanilla Bean Chocolates

²/₃ **cup heavy cream**
1 vanilla bean, split
9 ounces bittersweet chocolate, chopped
**1 tablespoon unsalted butter, room temperature,
    cut into pieces**
4 ounces bittersweet chocolate, melted, for coating
1 pound bittersweet chocolate, for tempering

1. **Line an 8-by-8-inch baking pan with plastic wrap, letting it overhang the edges on all sides.**

2. Combine cream and vanilla bean in a saucepan over medium-high heat and bring to a boil. Remove from heat, cover saucepan, and let steep for 15 minutes.

3. Place the chopped chocolate in a bowl.

4. Strain cream into a clean saucepan and bring to a boil again over medium-high heat.

5. Pour cream over chopped chocolate and wait 1 minute. Slowly stir with a wooden spoon or whisk until the chocolate is fully melted and combined with the cream.

6. Add butter and stir just until the mixture is smooth, thick, and uniform.

7. Pour the ganache into the prepared baking pan in a smooth, even layer. Let it set at room temperature until firm, 2 to 4 hours.

8. When you are ready to make the chocolates, line a couple of baking sheets with parchment paper or wax paper.

9. Using the plastic wrap as handles, remove the slab of ganache and flip it over onto a clean baking sheet or other work surface. Pull off the plastic wrap.

10. Using a small offset spatula, spread the melted 4 ounces of chocolate in a thin layer over the surface of the ganache slab. Let the chocolate set, about 20 minutes.

11. Flip the ganache slab. Using a sharp chef's knife, cut the slab into 1-inch squares. Refrigerate for a few minutes if the squares soften too much.

12. Line a few baking sheets with parchment or wax paper.

13. Melt and temper the 1 pound chocolate (page 17).

14. Dip the ganache squares in the tempered chocolate with a dipping fork, coating completely. Place dipped pieces on the baking sheets and let them set for 1 hour before decorating the tops or serving.

Yield: About 60 chocolates

Storage: Store in an airtight container in a cool, dry place for up to 1 week.

Jasmine Tea Chocolates

^{2}/$_3$ cup heavy cream
^{1}/$_2$ cup jasmine tea leaves, chopped fine
9 ounces bittersweet chocolate, chopped

1 tablespoon unsalted butter, room temperature,
   cut into pieces
4 ounces bittersweet chocolate, melted, for coating
1 pound bittersweet chocolate, for tempering

1. Line an 8-by-8-inch baking pan with plastic wrap,
    letting it overhang the edges of the pan on all sides.

2. Combine cream and jasmine tea leaves in a sauce-
    pan over medium-high heat and bring to a boil.
    Remove from heat, cover saucepan, and let steep
    for 15 minutes.

3. Meanwhile, put the chopped chocolate into a bowl.

4. Strain cream into a clean saucepan and bring to a
    boil again over medium-high heat.

5. Pour cream over chopped chocolate and wait
    1 minute. Stir with a wooden spoon or whisk
    until the chocolate is melted and combined with
    the cream.

6. Add the butter and stir until the mixture is smooth,
    thick, and uniform.

7. Pour the ganache into the prepared baking pan.
    Let it set at room temperature until firm, 2 to 4
    hours.

8. Make the chocolates per the rest of the recipe for vanilla bean chocolates, starting with step 8.

Yield: About 60 chocolates

Storage: Store in an airtight container in a cool, dry place for up to 1 week.

Ginger Chocolates

²/₃ cup heavy cream
1 tablespoon crystallized ginger, chopped fine
9 ounces bittersweet chocolate, chopped
1 tablespoon unsalted butter, room temperature, cut into pieces
4 ounces bittersweet chocolate, melted, for coating
1 pound bittersweet chocolate

1. Line an 8-by-8-inch baking pan with plastic wrap, letting it overhang the edges of the pan on all sides.

2. Combine cream and ginger pieces in a saucepan over medium-high heat and bring to a boil. Remove from heat, cover saucepan, and let steep 15 minutes.

3. Place the chopped chocolate into a bowl.

4. **Strain cream into a clean saucepan and bring to a boil again over medium-high heat.**

 5. **Pour cream over chopped chocolate and wait for 1 minute. Then stir with a wooden spoon or whisk until the chocolate is melted and combined with the cream.**

6. **Add the butter and stir just until the mixture is smooth, thick, and uniform.**

 7. **Pour the ganache into the baking pan. Let it set at room temperature until firm, 2 to 4 hours.**

8. **Make the chocolates per the rest of the recipe for vanilla bean chocolates, starting with step 8.**

Yield: About 60 chocolates

Storage: Store in an airtight container in a cool, dry place for up to 1 week.

 DIPPED TRUFFLES

General
Description: *Elegant, rich chocolate truffles are balls of ganache covered in thin shells of tempered chocolate.* They have come to symbolize luxury and quality like no other candy. In many parts of the world, a box of truffles is

considered de rigueur to ensure a lady's affections on Valentine's Day.

History:
The first **simple truffles** were meant to look like the earthy mushrooms of the same name. Today, most truffles have a ganache center enrobed in tempered chocolate that forms a perfectly round, crisp shell. Originally, truffle ganaches were simply a mixture of chocolate and cream, but most modern chocolatiers experiment with unusual and exotic flavor combinations, such as passion fruit, chili, or green tea.

Serving Suggestions:
Decorate the outsides of truffles to match the flavor inside or simply to distinguish between different varieties. Drizzle melted chocolate over the tops or roll the truffles in nuts, shredded coconut, or confectioners' sugar.

Candy-Making Notes:
The key to perfect truffles is making the ganache as smooth as possible. Be sure your chocolate is chopped into small pieces so that they will melt evenly. And watch the temperature of the melted chocolate; if it gets too hot, the fat in the cream or butter may separate. Whisk in the dairy slowly and carefully.

Recipes:
Rich Chocolate Truffles

$^2/_3$ cup heavy cream
8 ounces bittersweet chocolate, chopped

1 tablespoon unsalted butter, room temperature,
    cut into pieces
1 pound bittersweet chocolate
Cocoa powder for rolling, if desired

1. Place the chopped chocolate in a bowl.

2. Place cream in a saucepan over medium-high heat
   and bring to a boil.

3. Pour cream over the chocolate and wait 1 minute.
   Slowly stir with a wooden spoon or whisk until
   the chocolate is fully melted and combined with
   the cream.

4. Add butter and stir just until the mixture is
   smooth, thick, and uniform.

5. Pour the ganache into a baking pan. Let it set at
   room temperature until firm enough to scoop,
   2 to 4 hours.

6. When you are ready to make the truffles, line a
   few baking sheets with parchment or wax paper.

7. Scoop balls of ganache and place them onto baking
   sheets. Roll them slightly between your hands for
   a rounder shape. If they start to melt, place the
   baking sheet in the refrigerator for a few minutes.

8. **Melt and temper the chocolate (page 17).**

9. **Dip the ganache centers in the tempered chocolate with a dipping fork, coating completely. Roll them in cocoa powder or place them back on the baking sheet to set.**

Yield: About 40 truffles

Storage: Store in an airtight container in a cool, dry place for up to 1 week.

White Chocolate Lemon Truffles

8 ounces white chocolate, chopped
$^1/_3$ cup whipping cream
$1^1/_2$ teaspoon lemon extract
1 tablespoon unsalted butter, room temperature,
    cut into pieces
1 pound bittersweet or white chocolate
Grated lemon zest for decorating

1. **Place the chopped white chocolate in a bowl.**

2. **Place cream in a saucepan over medium-high heat and bring to a boil.**

3. **Pour cream over the chocolate and wait 1 minute. Slowly stir with a wooden spoon or whisk until**

the chocolate is fully melted and combined with the cream.

4. Add the lemon extract and butter and stir just until the mixture is smooth, thick, and uniform.

5. Pour the ganache into a baking pan. Let it set at room temperature until firm enough to scoop, 2 to 4 hours.

6. Make the truffles per the rest of the recipe for rich chocolate truffles, starting with step 6 (page 40).

Yield: About 40 truffles

Storage: Store in an airtight container in a cool, dry place for up to 1 week.

Raspberry Chocolate Truffles

1 cup fresh raspberries
1/4 cup sugar
2/3 cup heavy cream
12 ounces bittersweet chocolate, chopped
1 tablespoon unsalted butter, room temperature, cut into pieces
1 pound bittersweet chocolate

1. Combine raspberries and sugar in a food processor and puree until smooth. Strain puree into a saucepan and cook over medium heat for about 10 minutes until it thickens. Remove from heat.

2. Place the chopped chocolate in a bowl.

3. Place cream in a saucepan over medium-high heat and bring to a boil.

4. Pour cream over the chocolate and wait 1 minute. Slowly stir with a wooden spoon or whisk until the chocolate is melted and combined with the cream.

5. Add the raspberry puree and butter, and stir just until the mixture is smooth, thick, and uniform.

6. Pour the ganache into a baking pan. Let it set at room temperature until firm enough to scoop, 2 to 4 hours.

7. Make the truffles per the rest of the recipe for dark chocolate truffles, starting with step 6 (page 40).

Yield: About 40 truffles

Storage: Store in an airtight container in a cool, dry place for up to 1 week.

Mocha Truffles

²/₃ cup heavy cream
1 tablespoon instant espresso powder
8 ounces bittersweet chocolate, chopped
1 tablespoon coffee liqueur
2 teaspoons unsalted butter, room temperature,
    cut into pieces
1 pound bittersweet chocolate

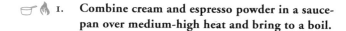 1.   Combine cream and espresso powder in a sauce-pan over medium-high heat and bring to a boil.

2.   Place the chopped chocolate in a bowl.

3.   Pour cream over chocolate and wait 1 minute. Stir with a wooden spoon or whisk until the chocolate is melted and combined with the cream.

4.   Add the coffee liqueur and butter and stir just until the mixture is smooth, thick, and uniform.

5.   Pour the ganache into a baking pan. Let it set at room temperature until firm enough to scoop, 2 to 4 hours.

6.   Make the truffles per the rest of the recipe for dark chocolate truffles, starting with step 6 (page 40).

Yield: About 40 truffles

⬢ Storage: Store in an airtight container in a cool, dry place for
            up to 1 week.

6a–d. ⬡   **FILLED MOLDED CHOCOLATES**

General   *The beautiful boxes you'll find at many candy shops*
Description: *contain delicate, jewel-like, filled molded chocolates.* A
            thin shell of tempered chocolate surrounds a variety
            of fruity, nutty, or chocolaty centers. These chocolates
            are characterized by their array of sleek geometric
            shapes and smooth, shiny finish. Sometimes the
            shape of the chocolate may give a clue to its filling,
            which makes choosing a chocolate a pleasurable
            guessing game.

History: Unlike truffles and other dipped chocolates, which
            are formed by *enrobing* (covering a candy center in
            tempered chocolate), molded filled chocolates are
            made by what is known as the *shell molding* process.
            Plastic molds in a variety of shapes are filled with a
            thin layer of tempered chocolate that dries to form
            a hollow shell ready to be filled with any number of
            delicious fillings, from caramel to fondant.

| Serving Suggestions: | With a variety of different fillings, you can make a personalized box of chocolates for a loved one. Filled molded chocolates are especially useful for soft, liquid fillings, such as caramel or fruit. |

| Candy-Making Notes: | Chocolate molds come in many classic and modern shapes, such as hearts, animals, and even vehicles. Simple shapes are easiest to fill evenly with chocolate and unmold without breaking. |

| Recipe: | **16 ounces bittersweet, semisweet, milk, or white chocolate** |

1. **Be sure the mold is completely clean and dry.**

2. **Melt and temper chocolate (page 17).**

3. **Ladle tempered chocolate into the mold, covering the surfaces of all the cavities.**

4. **Invert the mold over a clean baking sheet, letting excess chocolate run out until just a thin layer of chocolate remains.**

5. **Refrigerate the mold for 10 to 15 minutes.**

6. **When chocolate has set, add the filling of your choice (pages 47–50). Refrigerate for another 10 to 15 minutes to let filling set slightly.**

7. Ladle tempered chocolate over the top of the mold. Using an offset spatula, scrape off any excess chocolate, leaving the top of the mold completely clean and level. Refrigerate for 15 to 20 minutes.

8. When the chocolates look firm and are starting to shrink away from the sides of the mold, remove them from the refrigerator. Invert mold onto clean surface to unmold the chocolates.

Yield: About 35 filled chocolates

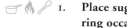 Storage: Store in an airtight container in a cool, dry place for up to 2 weeks.

Variations: **Caramel Filling**

$^3/_4$ cup sugar
$^2/_3$ cup heavy cream
4 tablespoons unsalted butter, room temperature, cut into pieces

1. Place sugar in a saucepan over medium heat, stirring occasionally until the sugar melts.

2. Continue cooking without stirring until the sugar turns a golden color, about 8 minutes.

3. While the sugar is cooking, heat the cream in a

saucepan over medium heat until it begins to simmer. Keep the cream warm, but don't let it boil.

4. Remove saucepan with sugar from heat and slowly pour in the hot cream, swirling to combine. The mixture will bubble up; let it settle slightly before adding more cream.

5. Add butter and stir to combine.

6. Let caramel cool to room temperature before using.

Mint Ganache Filling

²/₃ cup heavy cream
¹/₂ cup mint leaves, chopped fine
6 ounces bittersweet chocolate
2 teaspoons unsalted butter, room temperature, cut into pieces

1. Combine cream and mint leaves in a saucepan over medium-high heat and bring to a boil. Remove from heat, cover, and let steep for 10 minutes.

2. Place the chopped chocolate in a bowl.

3. Strain cream into a clean saucepan and bring to a boil again over medium-high heat.

4. Pour cream over chocolate and wait 1 minute. Slowly stir with a wooden spoon or whisk until the chocolate is melted and combined with the cream.

5. Add butter and stir just until the mixture is smooth, thick, and uniform.

6. Let ganache cool to room temperature before using.

Kirsch Ganache Filling

6 ounces bittersweet chocolate, chopped
$^2/_3$ cup heavy cream
1 tablespoon kirsch or other liqueur

1. Place the chocolate in a bowl.

2. Place cream in a saucepan over medium-high heat and bring to a boil.

3. Pour cream over chocolate and wait 1 minute. Slowly stir with a wooden spoon or whisk until the chocolate is fully melted and combined with the cream.

4. Add the kirsch and stir just until the mixture is smooth, thick, and uniform.

5. Let ganache cool to room temperature before using.

Praline Ganache Filling

$^1/_2$ cup hazelnut praline (page 252)
6 ounces bittersweet chocolate, chopped
$^2/_3$ cup heavy cream

1. Place the praline in a food processor and process until very fine, almost a paste.

2. Place the chocolate in a bowl.

3. Place cream in a saucepan over medium-high heat and bring to a boil.

4. Pour cream over chocolate and wait 1 minute. Slowly stir with a wooden spoon or whisk until the chocolate is fully melted and combined with the cream.

5. Add the praline and stir until the mixture is smooth, thick, and uniform.

6. Let ganache cool to room temperature before using.

7a–b.

HOLLOW MOLDED CHOCOLATES

General Description: *Hollow molded chocolates are three-dimensional shells of chocolate, perfectly and elaborately detailed on the outside and hollow on the inside.* A child biting the ear off a chocolate Easter bunny discovers the pleasure of crunching through a crisp layer of chocolate to find the hollow center. Hollow molded chocolates come in a variety of novelty shapes like **solid molded chocolates**, but they are made like **filled molded chocolates**.

History:

The earliest chocolate molds were expertly handmade and elaborately detailed in France and Germany. Many of these beautifully detailed antique molds are now collectors' items. Most giant molded chocolates, such as bunnies or Santas, are hollow.

Serving Suggestions:

Chocolate bunnies are the most popular hollow molded chocolate, but almost any three-dimensional mold can be used to make a hollow chocolate. Use your hollow chocolates as containers for other sweets.

Candy-Making Notes:

The key to making hollow molded chocolates is rotating the mold to coat all parts evenly. Get the melted chocolate into the most difficult-to-reach corners first, while the chocolate is still fairly liquid.

Recipe:

16 ounces bittersweet, semisweet, or milk chocolate

1. **Make sure the mold is completely clean and dry.**

2. **Melt and temper the chocolate (page 17).**

3.   Ladle tempered chocolate into the mold, covering the surfaces of all the cavities.

4.   Invert the mold over a clean baking sheet, letting excess chocolate run out until just a thin layer of chocolate remains.

5.   Refrigerate the mold to let the chocolate set, 10 to 15 minutes, depending on the size of the mold.

6.   When the chocolate shells look firm and are starting to shrink away from the sides of the mold, remove from the refrigerator. Flip mold onto clean surface to unmold chocolate shells.

7.   To join the two shells, warm a clean baking sheet in the oven. Press the open side of one shell to the sheet until the rim starts to melt.

8.   Quickly press the two shells together and hold until the chocolate sets.

Yield: One large hollow chocolate

Storage: Store in an airtight container at room temperature for up to 1 week.

Variation:

Hollow Easter Egg with Treats
Use a three-dimensional Easter egg mold with two half shells. Follow the recipe through step 6. Then fill one of the half shells with Easter candies of your choice: jellybeans, foil-wrapped chocolate eggs, marshmallows, or candy eggs. You can then place the other half shell on top and seal it shut (steps 7 and 8).

8a–b.

MENDIANTS

General Description:

Mendiants made of dark chocolate studded with nuts and dried fruits are one of France's most colorful and elegant confections. Tempered chocolate is poured into small disks and then sprinkled with chopped nuts and other goodies. The traditional toppings for mendiants are almonds, hazelnuts, dried figs, and raisins, which correspond to the colors of the robes worn by the Roman Catholic religious orders of Carmelites, Augustinians, Franciscans, and Dominicans.

History:

Mendiant means "beggar" in French, and these candies derive their name from *mendicant*, the name of the French religious order that vows poverty and relies on the charity of others to survive. Mendiant candies originated in Provence, where the four nuts and fruits were served as part of the 13 Desserts of Christmas: Thirteen simple sweets symbolizing Jesus and his 12 apostles.

Serving Suggestions: ❄ 🎀	Mendiants are a beautiful addition to the holiday table, and they are traditionally served at Christmastime.
Candy-Making Notes:	Create an interesting combination of colors, flavors, and textures using your favorite nuts and fruits. Try almonds, hazelnuts, raisins, and dried figs or pistachios, cranberries, orange peel, almonds, and golden raisins.
Recipe:	**1 pound bittersweet chocolate 1 cup dried fruits and nuts**

1. **Line several baking sheets with parchment paper or silicone baking mats.**

2. **Melt and temper the chocolate (page 17).**

3. **Drop small spoonfuls of tempered chocolate onto the baking sheets. The chocolate should spread into circles; use the spoon to fix any misshapen rounds.**

4. **Gently place toppings on each chocolate round. Let set for 1 hour.**

Yield:	About 40 mendiants
Storage:	Store in an airtight container in a cool, dry place for up to 2 weeks.

Variation: **White Chocolate Mendiants**

White chocolate provides a dramatic background for darker mendiant toppings such as cranberries, dried cherries, or cocoa nibs.

9.   **MINT MELTAWAYS**

General
Description:

The name of this confection describes the exquisite sensation of popping one in your mouth. Meltaways are made of chocolate and fats such as cocoa butter or coconut oil, covered in a thin chocolate shell. The resulting confection is smooth and velvety, and it softens quickly under heat, creating the melt-in-your-mouth sensation.

History:

The most famous mint meltaways are Frango Mint Chocolates. The name and original recipe were created by Frederick and Nelson's department store in Seattle. In 1929 the store was acquired by Marshall Field's of Chicago, and the chocolate-making operation was moved to the Windy City, where the mint meltaways quickly became an iconic item for the store.

Serving
Suggestions:

Meltaways are traditionally dipped in tempered chocolate, but you can simply wrap them in colored foil or dust them with confectioners' sugar.

Candy-Making
Notes:
⚠

You can use coconut oil instead of cocoa butter, but be sure that is it is a food-grade ingredient, not a beauty product that might contain additives.

Recipe:

¹/₄ cup cocoa butter
12 ounces semisweet chocolate
¹/₂ teaspoon peppermint extract
10 ounces bittersweet chocolate or coating chocolate

1. **Line an 8-by-8-inch baking pan with foil and grease well.**

2. **Warm cocoa butter in a metal bowl set over a pot of simmering water, stirring occasionally, until it is liquid.**

3. **Add the chocolate and heat until it has melted, stirring to combine.**

4. **Remove from heat and stir in the peppermint extract.**

5. **Pour mixture into the baking pan. Refrigerate overnight or until firm.**

6. **Turn out onto a clean baking sheet. Using a sharp knife, cut into 1-inch squares. Wrap in foil, dust in**

confectioners' sugar, or dip in chocolate as in
steps 7 to 9.

7. Line a couple of baking sheets with parchment
or wax paper.

8. Melt and temper the chocolate (page 17) or melt
coating chocolate.

9. Dip the squares in the chocolate with a dipping
fork, coating completely. Place dipped pieces on
baking sheets to set for 1 hour before serving.

Yield: About 48 mints

Storage: Store in an airtight container in a cool, dry place for
up to 2 weeks.

10. **PEPPERMINT PATTIES**

General
Description: *With their thin, dark chocolate shells covering a pure
white, mint-flavored filling, peppermint patties are
as refreshing as crisp winter air.* These small, puck-
shaped candies are beloved for their intense peppermint flavor, as well as the contrast between the crisp
chocolate coating and the soft, creamy center. Recipes
for peppermint patties vary; some have a true fondant
filling, whereas others call for mixing confectioners'

sugar and butter or whipped egg whites and confectioners' sugar. However, the filling should always be smooth and give easily under the bite, never hard or liquid.

History:

The most famous version of this candy is the York Peppermint Pattie, with its iconic silver foil wrapping. It was originally produced in 1940 by the York Cone Company in York, Pennsylvania, hence its name. The first peppermint patties had firm centers, but today the centers are soft.

Serving Suggestions:

Peppermint patties are a Christmastime classic, but wrapped in brightly colored foil they make a welcome addition to the Halloween candy bowl. Use heart-shaped cookie cutters for Valentine's Day mints.

Candy-Making Notes:

It's best to use a good-quality peppermint oil, because mild extracts will not provide the trademark intense minty flavor for which these candies are known.

Recipe:

1 egg white
4 cups confectioners' sugar
$^1/_3$ cup light corn syrup
$^1/_2$ teaspoon peppermint oil or extract
Cornstarch for dusting
1 pound bittersweet or coating chocolate, chopped

1. **Line two baking sheets with parchment paper.**

2. In a stand mixer with the whisk attachment, whisk the egg white on medium speed until it is stiff and forms peaks.

3. Slowly add the confectioners' sugar while whisking on medium speed.

4. Add the corn syrup and peppermint oil and knead the mixture with your hands until it has the smooth consistency of dough.

5. On a surface lightly dusted with cornstarch, roll the dough to $1/4$ inch thick. Use a $2^1/2$-inch round cookie cutter to cut out circles of dough. Place them on baking sheets and refrigerate until firm, about 45 minutes.

6. Line a few baking sheets with parchment or wax paper. Melt and temper chocolate (page 17).

7. Dip each patty into the chocolate to coat completely. Place patties on baking sheets to set for about 1 hour.

Yield: About 20 candies

Storage: Store in a cool, dry place in an airtight container for up to 2 weeks.

11a–b.   **ROCHERS**

General
Description:

Not to be confused with the commercially made Italian candy Ferrero Rocher, rochers are a classic candy made of chocolate-coated nuts. Slivered almonds are coated in sugar and roasted, then dipped in melted chocolate and formed into rough clusters. Rochers are traditionally found in fine French chocolate shops alongside **truffles** and **filled molded chocolates**, but they are much easier to make, making them a fine choice for the beginning chocolatier.

History:

Rocher means "rock" in French, aptly describing the craggy appearance of this candy. Rochers may have evolved as a version of **dragées** or as yet another way French confectioners combined chocolate and nuts. The word *rocher* also refers to two other rustically shaped sweet confections in France: roughly piped meringues flavored with chocolate and almond and sweet coconut cookies that resemble American coconut macaroons.

Serving
Suggestions:

Rochers can be made with different nuts and chocolates. Try milk or white chocolate with hazelnuts. For a very French chocolate tray, serve rochers with **mendiants** and **truffles**.

Candy-Making
Notes:

Keeping the clusters small makes them easier to dip. Smaller clusters are also easier to form into mounds.

Recipe: **2 cups slivered almonds**
1 tablespoon vanilla extract or kirsch liqueur
1 cup sugar
8 ounces bittersweet chocolate

1. **Preheat the oven to 350°F. Line a baking sheet with parchment paper or a silicone baking mat.**

2. **Combine the almonds and vanilla extract in a bowl, stirring until the nuts are moistened.**

3. **Add sugar and toss until the nuts are coated.**

4. **Spread the nuts in a single layer on the baking sheet. Toast in the oven for 5 to 10 minutes until the sugar has melted and caramelized around the nuts, occasionally turning the nuts with a metal spatula.**

5. **Remove from oven and let cool for a few minutes.**

6. **Line a baking sheet with parchment paper or a silicone baking mat.**

7. **Melt and temper the chocolate (page 17).**

8. **Spoon a small amount of nuts into the chocolate, toss to coat evenly, and then spoon them onto the baking sheet in neat 2-inch clusters.**

Yield:	About 24 nut clusters
Storage:	Store in an airtight container between sheets of wax paper for up to 2 weeks.
Variation:	***Coconut Rochers*** If you are a fan of **coconut-and-almond candy**, this version is sure to please. Coconut adds extra richness and chewy texture to rochers. Add $1/2$ cup shredded unsweetened coconut to the nuts in step 3.

12. SIMPLE TRUFFLES

General Description:	*Who could have imagined that the truffle—a rare, highly prized fungus—could inspire a chocolate confection?* Chocolate truffles are little balls of ganache dipped in tempered chocolate or rolled in cocoa powder. They owe their origin to the truffle, a type of mushroom famous for its earthy flavor. Chocolate truffles are widely considered the best form of chocolate, just as truffles are considered the best variety of mushroom. Simple truffles consist of nothing more than chocolate and cream. They are smooth and velvety, capturing the essence of chocolate.
History:	Chocolate truffles originated in France, which is not surprising, given that France is a major source of black truffles as well as pastries and confections. The

first truffles were created in the 1920s and were a simple ganache of chocolate and cream. They were deliberately roughly shaped and rolled in cocoa powder to enhance their resemblance to their namesake. Although truffles have evolved into a more refined, sophisticated form (see **dipped truffles**), the simpler, rustic truffle has made a comeback in recent years as a straightforward way to enjoy very good chocolate.

Serving Suggestions:

You can experiment with different varieties of chocolate to compare flavors. Serve these truffles after dinner with wine. Different wines pair better with different chocolates, but most red wines, such as cabernet sauvignon or Beaujolais, or fortified desserts wines, such as port or Banyuls, complement dark chocolates.

Candy-Making Notes:

This recipe is for basic truffles similar to the original French truffles. They are easy to make and do not require tempering chocolate. Unlike **dipped truffles**, which are perfectly round, these truffles can be more casually and naturally shaped. Don't worry if your truffles are slightly irregular—that's precisely how they should be.

Recipe:

1¹/₂ pounds semisweet or bittersweet chocolate, finely chopped

1 cup cream

³/₄ teaspoon vanilla extract

¹/₂ cup cocoa powder for rolling

1. Line an 8-by-8-inch baking pan with foil and grease well. Place chopped chocolate in a metal bowl.

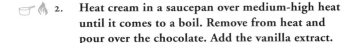 2. Heat cream in a saucepan over medium-high heat until it comes to a boil. Remove from heat and pour over the chocolate. Add the vanilla extract.

3. Let sit for 1 to 2 minutes; then gently whisk the mixture until it is fully blended. It should be smooth and glossy.

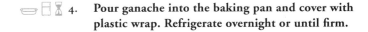 4. Pour ganache into the baking pan and cover with plastic wrap. Refrigerate overnight or until firm.

5. When you are ready to make the truffles, remove the pan of ganache from the refrigerator. Line a baking sheet with parchment paper. Fill a small bowl with the cocoa powder.

6. Using a melon baller or spoon, scoop small portions of the ganache and roll into balls between your hands. Roll in the cocoa powder to coat and place on the baking sheet to set.

Yield: About 48 truffles

Storage: Store in an airtight container at room temperature for up to 5 days. Because they are not dipped in tempered chocolate, these truffles will not last long.

13.   **SOLID MOLDED CHOCOLATES**

General
Description:

One of the most creative applications of tempered chocolate is casting it into elaborately detailed shapes. Some molded chocolates are flat-backed, whereas others are fully three-dimensional. These confections are the ultimate in chocolate art, and most children—as well as many adults—will agree that chocolate tastes much better when it's shaped like a bunny.

History:

The first chocolate molds were made of metal, usually tin, in 19th-century France. Germany soon became a productive chocolate-mold maker since the country already had a large industry making similar molds for shaping cookies. Many of these beautifully detailed molds are now collectors' items. The chocolate bunny likely originated in Germany, along with the Easter bunny, who is known as the *Osterhase*, or Easter hare.

Serving
Suggestions:

Molds of all shapes and sizes are available in cooking supply stores and online, which makes it easy to custom-design chocolate for any event: Halloween pumpkins, spring flowers, wedding bells. Many flat-backed molds also allow you to add a lollipop stick for chocolate lollipops. Decorate the finished chocolates by tying ribbons around the necks of chocolate bunnies, using edible paints to add color, or using small candies to simulate buttons or eyes.

| Candy-Making Notes: | This recipe can be used for making flat-backed solid chocolates or three-dimensional solid chocolates. Some three-dimensional molds are specially made as one piece. Unless you invest in the sturdy, plastic, professional-quality molds, it may be difficult to make solid chocolate pieces that are more than 24-inches tall; the molds may not be strong enough to hold the weight of so much melted chocolate. Use extra-large molds for **hollow molded chocolates**. |

Recipe: **16 ounces bittersweet, semisweet, or milk chocolate**

1. **Make sure the mold is completely clean and dry.**

2. **Melt and temper chocolate (page 17).**

3. **Ladle tempered chocolate into the mold cavities, filling them just to the top. Tap the mold lightly on the counter to eliminate air bubbles.**

4. **Using an offset spatula, scrape away any extra chocolate, leaving the top of the mold completely clean and level.**

5. **Refrigerate the mold for 15 to 30 minutes to let the chocolate set.**

6. **When the chocolate looks firm and is starting to**

shrink away from the sides of the mold, remove it from the refrigerator. Flip it over on a clean surface to unmold chocolates. At this point, you are finished if you are making flat-backed chocolates.

7. To join two halves, warm a clean baking sheet in the oven. Press the flat side of one half to the sheet just until the surface starts to melt.

8. Quickly press the half to the other to join. Hold it together until the chocolate sets.

Yield: One large chocolate

Storage: Store in an airtight container at room temperature for up to 1 week.

Fruits and Jellies

14. **AGAR JELLIES**

General
Description:

Asia's version of Jell-O is made with agar, an ingredient made from seaweed with properties similar to gelatin. Like Western-style jelly candies, agar jellies come in a variety of colors, flavors, and forms. The texture of agar jellies is somewhat firmer and chewier than gelatin-based jellies. Commercially made agar-based candies are commonly sold in stores across Asia. One of the most popular styles is rainbow-colored cubes, made of thin layers of variously colored jelly. Opaque varieties are also popular, made with coconut milk or almond milk.

History:

The word *agar agar* means "jelly" in Malay; either *agar* or *agar agar* can be used to refer to the substance. Agar has been used across Asia for centuries as a thickener in desserts as well as sauces and soups. It was brought to North America in the 19th century and has become popular as a gelatin substitute, especially since it contains no animal products. One form of agar jelly popular in Asia is an almond-flavored type called *almond tofu*, due to the similarities in appearance and texture.

Serving
Suggestions:

Agar jellies can be made like gelatin-based **fruit
jellies**. It is usually served with mixed fruit as a
simple, light dessert.

Candy-Making
Notes:

Agar can be substituted for gelatin in almost all
recipes, making it an invaluable ingredient for people
with vegetarian or kosher dietary requirements. It can
be found in Asian groceries in dried strips or in powdered form similar to powdered gelatin. Agar-based
jellies have a denser texture than gelatin-based jellies.

Recipe:

2 cups almond milk
$^1/_2$ cup milk
$^1/_4$ cup sugar
$2^1/_2$ teaspoons powdered agar
$^1/_2$ teaspoon almond extract
Food coloring, if desired

1. **Set aside a 6-by-6-inch baking pan or individual
dessert bowls.**

2. **Combine almond milk, milk, sugar, and agar in a
saucepan over medium heat, stirring occasionally,
until the sugar dissolves.**

3. **Bring to a boil and cook for about 5 minutes.**

4. **Remove from heat and stir in almond extract and
food coloring, if desired.**

5. **Pour mixture into baking pan or individual dessert bowls. Refrigerate until it has fully set before serving.**

 6. **Cut jelly into 1-inch cubes or other shapes.**

Yield: About 36 cubes

Storage: Refrigerate in an airtight container for up to 1 week.

 15. **APPLE JELLIES**

General Description: *Like a cross between Jell-O and **pâtes de fruits**, apple jellies are chunky, slightly chewy squares bursting with fruit flavor.* Made with applesauce and gelatin and often studded with nuts, these jellies taste naturally sweet. Apple jellies are popular in the American Northwest, particularly in Washington, famous for its apple production. Commercial apple jellies called Aplets & Cotlets are produced in Washington. These rectangular blocks of jelly candy come in apple and apricot flavors studded with walnuts and liberally dusted with confectioners' sugar.

History: Apples are one of the key crops of Washington; they were declared the state fruit in 1989. It is not surprising that Aplets & Cotlets were invented in apple country. They were created by two

Armenians, Armen Tertsagian and Mark Balaban, who immigrated to Washington in the early 1900s. The two men grew apples at their farm, Liberty Orchards. The dilemma of how to deal with surplus apple crops in the years following World War I inspired them to create an apple-flavored, American version of **Turkish delight**.

Serving
Suggestions:
❆ ☀ ☁ ❆

Like Turkish delight, these candies make festive holiday treats. They are also ideal to make in the fall during apple season.

Candy-Making
Notes:

Use a good-quality applesauce that is thick and contains as few additives as possible; it will cook better and give the candies a purer taste and texture. You can also make your own applesauce for these candies; be sure to use tart, firm apples and cook the applesauce until it is thick.

Recipe:
1 cup unsweetened applesauce
1¼ cups sugar
1½ tablespoons gelatin
1 tablespoon lemon juice
1 cup walnuts
Confectioners' sugar for dusting

1. **Grease an 8-by-8-inch pan with butter or cooking spray.**

2.   **Combine applesauce and sugar in a saucepan and bring to boil over medium heat, stirring occasionally to prevent burning. Continue cooking on medium-low heat for about 10 minutes until the applesauce is thick.**

3.   **Dissolve the gelatin in ¹/₂ cup cold water. Add it to the apple mixture and stir to combine. Cook for about 5 minutes.**

4.   **Add lemon juice and walnuts and stir to combine.**

5.   **Pour into prepared baking pan and let cool and set overnight.**

6.   **Using a sharp, well-oiled knife, cut into 1-inch squares and roll in confectioners' sugar to coat.**

Yield: About 64 jellies

Storage: Store in an airtight container between sheets of wax paper for up to 2 weeks.

 CANDIED CITRUS PEEL

General Description: *Also called* citrus confit *or* candied citron, *these thin strips of citrus peel preserved in sugar are a common Christmas confection.* Orange and lemon peel are the most common, but any citrus will do. The peel is cooked in a sugar syrup until softened and sweetened, rolled in granulated sugar, and sometimes even dipped in chocolate; candied orange peels dipped in chocolate are called *orangettes*. This versatile candy is served as a snack or used as an ingredient in desserts such as fruitcake, panettone, and plum pudding.

History: Candying was developed in ancient times to preserve fresh fruit. It was first practiced in Asia and the Middle East, and it travelled to Europe in the 8th century along with the spread of sugar. Candied fruit and citrus peel add flavor to cakes and breads, especially holiday desserts such as fruitcake, lebkuchen, and stollen. At the end of the year, these pastries filled with candied fruit and citrus peel are a sweet reminder of the abundance of summer and fall.

Serving Suggestions: Candied citrus peels are a traditional Christmas treat. They can be chopped into pieces and sprinkled into cake or cookie batter or used as a garnish for truffles and tarts. Candied citrus peel is also used in **panforte de Siena** and **sugarplums** and can be sprinkled over **chocolate bark** or into **chocolate bars**.

Candy-Making Notes: Almost any citrus can be used in this recipe, such as oranges, lemons, tangerines, or grapefruits. The blanching process sweetens and softens the bitter citrus peel.

Recipe: **4 oranges or other citrus fruits**
2 cups sugar
Extra sugar for rolling

1.   **Cut the oranges into quarters, then cut off the peel, leaving a thin layer of pith. You can eat the fruit or use it in another recipe.**

2.   **Slice the peel into thin strips about ¹/₂ inch wide.**

3.   **To blanch the peels, place them in a saucepan and fill it with enough water to cover them (about 1¹/₂ cups). Bring to a boil over medium-high heat for 1 minute.**

4.   **Drain, cover the peels with fresh water, and bring to a boil again. Repeat this process once more, for a total of 3 blanchings.**

5.   **Combine sugar and water in a clean saucepan over medium-high heat and bring to boil.**

6.   **Add the peels and reduce heat to medium or medium-low to keep the syrup at a simmer. Let the peels soak for 45–60 minutes, until they look almost translucent.**

7.   **Remove from heat, and pour the peels and syrup into a container to cool.**

8. **Take the candied peels out of the syrup and place them on a wire rack to drain the excess syrup. Roll them in granulated sugar for a sparkling appearance.**

Yield: About 5 dozen peels

Storage: Before being rolled in sugar, citrus peels can be stored up to 3 months in the syrup if covered and refrigerated. After rolling them in sugar, store them in an airtight container at room temperature for up to 1 week.

Variation: ***Orangettes***
Candied citrus peel dipped in chocolate is an elegant and simple holiday gift. The tartness of the peel goes especially well with bittersweet chocolate.

Line a baking sheet with wax paper. Melt and temper 1 pound bittersweet chocolate. Dip each candied orange peel halfway into the chocolate and lay it on the prepared sheet. Let set until firm, about 1 hour.

17. **CANDIED FRUIT**

General
Description: *Glistening candied fruits capture nature's bounty at its peak.* Soaking fruits in sugar syrup saturates them with sugar, replacing their water content with sweetness and rendering them sweet and plump while

retaining their fruity flavor. The high concentration of sugar preserves the fruit and prevents the growth of mold. Also known as *glacé fruit* or *crystallized fruit*, these confections are beautiful delicacies. Whole candied fruits such as pineapples and melons, are prized for their size, beauty, and succulence; chopped candied fruits are irreplaceable in plum pudding and fruitcake; and candied slices of citrus are a great way to decorate tarts and cakes.

History:

The art of candying fruit began 4,000 years ago in Egypt as a way to preserve fresh, ripe fruit. Many ancient cultures, such as the Romans, Arabs, and Chinese, realized that storing fruits and other foods in honey or sugar syrup helps them last longer. Once candying fruit became popular in Europe, the technique was refined until it became a confectioner's art. Candying fruit continues to be a cherished tradition in Europe, particularly France, Spain, and Portugal.

Serving Suggestions:

A jar of candied orange slices makes a gorgeous and thoughtful holiday gift: The fruit can be slowly enjoyed over the winter months, and the syrup can be used to add extra flavor to baked goods.

Candy-Making Notes:

This simplified home method is much quicker than the traditional method of candying fruits, and it has equally delicious results. Other sliced fruits can be used instead of oranges.

Candied Orange Slices

Recipe: **$1/2$ cup sugar**
I orange
Extra sugar for coating

1. **Combine sugar and $1^1/2$ cup water in a saucepan and bring to a boil.**

2. **While you are waiting for the mixture to boil, cut the orange in half and then into $1/4$-inch slices.**

3. **Add the orange slices to the boiling sugar syrup and cook on medium-low heat, flipping the slices occasionally, for 40 to 50 minutes until the orange slices are translucent and soft but still intact.**

4. **Place a wire rack over a baking pan to catch drips. Use a slotted spoon to transfer the orange slices to the wire rack to cool and dry overnight.**

5. **Place the extra sugar in a bowl. Dredge orange slices in the sugar to coat.**

Yield: About 20 slices

Storage: Refrigerate in an airtight container between sheets of wax paper. If protected from heat, candied fruit can last as long as 6 months.

18.   **CANDY APPLES**

**General
Description:**

Candy apples, or toffee apples, *are apples dipped in a sweet, cinnamon-flavored sugar syrup with a wooden stick inserted into each core as a convenient handle.* The sugar syrup is tinted red and dries to a hard coating, enhancing the candylike appearance. Candy apples are associated with Halloween and commonly found at fairs and carnivals, especially in the United Kingdom and North America. Their distinctive hue led to the color name "candy apple red."

History:

Although candied fruit and candied apples date back to ancient times, the candy apple as we know it likely originated in Britain in the late 19th century. The first candy apples made in Britain were sold at local fairs.

**Serving
Suggestions:**

Candy apples are wonderful treats to make for local carnivals or festivals. You can roll them in toppings, such as chopped nuts or sprinkles, before the candy coating dries.

**Candy-Making
Notes:**

The sugar for this recipe must be cooked to 300°F, or hard crack, which is likely the highest temperature you will see in a candy recipe. Be very careful when dipping the apples in the hot syrup.

Recipe: 12 apples
12 craft sticks or skewers
2 cups sugar
1 cup light corn syrup
1 drop cinnamon oil
Few drops red food coloring, if desired

1.   Wash apples and remove the stems. Insert a wooden craft stick or skewer about 2 inches into the core of each apple.

2.   Line several baking sheets with wax paper or silicone baking mats.

3.   Combine sugar, corn syrup, and $^1/_2$ cup water in a saucepan and bring to a boil over medium-high heat. Continue cooking until the mixture reaches 300°F, hard crack stage. Remove saucepan from heat and stir in cinnamon oil and red food coloring.

4.   Dip apples one at a time into the syrup. Roll in toppings if desired. Place on the baking sheets to firm up before serving.

Yield: 12 candy apples

Storage: Store at room temperature for up to 2 days.

CARAMEL APPLES

General Description:	*Bright red apples that have been stuck on sticks and covered in creamy caramel and nuts are a common sight at Halloween.* Caramel apples are simply apples that have been dipped in a sweet caramel sauce and skewered on a wooden stick for ease of eating. They can be dipped in chocolate and rolled in nuts, sprinkles, and other toppings.
History:	Caramel apples are a more recent invention than **candy apples**. The first recipe for caramel apples was printed on bags of Kraft's caramel candies in the 1950s. A Kraft sales representative named Dan Walker is credited with inventing the recipe or creating home kits for making caramel apples, undoubtedly boosting sales of his company's products in the process. Caramel apples are traditionally associated with Halloween and harvest time.
Serving Suggestions:	It is easy to roll dipped apples in a variety of coatings, from nuts to grated coconut to crushed candies. Set out dishes of different coatings and let guests make their own versions.
Candy-Making Notes:	Whereas the bright red, mild Red Delicious apple may be the most popular choice for making caramel apples, tarter varieties offer a better contrast to the sweet, buttery caramel. Try Granny Smith, McIntosh,

or Gala. Small lady apples make for a charming variation.

Recipe: **12 apples**
12 wooden sticks
$^3/_4$ cup sugar
$^1/_4$ cup light corn syrup
1 cup heavy cream
1$^1/_2$ tablespoons unsalted butter
$^1/_2$ teaspoon vanilla extract

1. **Wash the apples and remove the stems. Insert a wooden stick into the core of each apple.**

2. **Line several baking sheets with wax paper or silicone baking mats.**

3. **Combine sugar, corn syrup, cream, and butter in a saucepan. Bring to a boil over medium-high heat. Continue cooking until the mixture reaches 245°F, soft ball stage.**

4. **Remove saucepan from heat and stir in the vanilla extract. Let caramel cool for a few minutes.**

5. **Dip apples one at a time into the caramel. Roll in toppings as desired. Place on baking sheets to firm up before serving.**

Yield:	12 caramel apples
Storage:	Refrigerate for up to 2 days.
Variation:	***Caramel Apples Dipped in Chocolate and Toppings*** Let caramel apples sit for 1 minute before dipping them in melted chocolate and then rolling them in sprinkles, nuts, or crushed candies.

20.   **CHOCOLATE-COVERED CHERRIES**

General Description:	*Chocolate-covered cherries are distinct from other chocolate-dipped fruit because they are made by dipping maraschino cherries in fondant and then in chocolate.* They must rest for a week so that the fondant can reliquefy, combining with the cherry to form a sweet, sugary center. The chocolate covering remains solid, allowing for the experience of biting through the hard outer shell to a rich, liquid filling. Cherries that are only dipped in chocolate, without the fondant covering, are called *chocolate-dipped cherries*.
History:	The first chocolate-covered cherries are attributed to Cella's Confections, which began making them in 1929. Cella's Confections is located on Canal Street in New York City, which became famous in the 19th century for being home to many candy factories.

Today, the company is the only one that remains, and their chocolate-covered cherries are still popular.

Serving
Suggestions:

If you are able to get maraschino cherries with the stems, they will make for a stunning presentation. You can also soak cherries in kirsch or other liqueur before dipping.

Candy-Making
Notes:

When dipping the cherries in the chocolate, make sure each one is completely covered in chocolate so that the fondant will not leak when it liquefies.

Recipe:

1 pound maraschino cherries
2¹/₂ cups confectioners' sugar, sifted
¹/₄ cup unsalted butter, room temperature
1 tablespoon corn syrup
1 teaspoon kirsch liqueur, optional
2 pounds bittersweet chocolate

1. **Drain cherries, reserving the syrup in a covered container. Refrigerate syrup until ready to use.**

2. **Place cherries on a rack set over a baking sheet to dry overnight.**

3. **Make the fondant: In a stand mixer, beat the butter until smooth and creamy. Add confectioners' sugar 1 cup at a time, and beat until it forms a smooth dough that is not sticky.**

4.   Add corn syrup and 1½ tablespoons of the
     reserved cherry liquid, and mix until combined.
     Add kirsch and mix until combined.

5.   Pinch off a small piece of the fondant and form it
     into a ball. Flatten it into a disc and place a cherry
     in the center. Wrap the fondant around the cherry
     to fully encase it.

6.   Repeat with the remaining cherries. Place the
     cherries on a baking sheet and refrigerate over-
     night until the fondant is completely firm.

7.   When you're ready to dip the cherries, melt and
     temper the chocolate (page 17). Line a baking
     sheet with parchment paper or wax paper.

8.   Dip the cherries in the chocolate and place on the
     prepared sheet. Refrigerate the dipped cherries for
     about 1 hour until the chocolate has set.

9.   Place the cherries in an airtight container and
     store for 1 week before serving.

Yield: About 60 cherries

Storage: Storage is the key to delicious chocolate-covered cher-
          ries; the centers need a week to liquefy. Refrigerate in
          an airtight container for up to 3 weeks.

21a–b.   **CHOCOLATE-DIPPED STRAWBERRIES**

General
Description:

Strawberries and chocolate have long been associated with romance. Although dark chocolate is classically used for dipping, white chocolate is also popular. Strawberries can be double-dipped in different chocolates for visual contrast. One striking variation is *tuxedo strawberries*: The berries are dipped first in white chocolate, then in dark chocolate on both sides to create a "V" resembling men's formal wear. Chocolate-dipped strawberries can also be drizzled with chocolate in abstract designs.

History:

It is unknown who invented the chocolate-dipped strawberry; it could be a natural extension of **candied fruit** or **chocolate fondue**.

Serving
Suggestions:

This classic aphrodisiac can be served with a flute of champagne on Valentine's Day. Elegant chocolate-dipped strawberries are often found at wedding parties and formal dinner buffets.

Candy-Making
Notes:

You will get the best results from using tempered chocolate, but untempered chocolate will also work. The untempered coating will be soft, like chocolate fondue, whereas tempered chocolate will form a firm, crisp shell. Keep strawberries made with untempered chocolate in the refrigerator if the weather is warm.

Recipe: **20 fresh strawberries, washed and dried**
16 ounces bittersweet chocolate

1. **Line a baking sheet with parchment or wax paper. Make sure the strawberries are completely dry.**

2. **Melt and temper the chocolate (page 17), or simply melt the chocolate.**

3. **Holding strawberries by the stem, dip them into the chocolate one at a time, covering about three-quarters of each berry.**

4. **Allow excess chocolate to run off before placing each dipped strawberry on the baking sheet.**

5. **Let chocolate set before dipping in a contrasting chocolate, drizzling with more chocolate, or serving.**

Yield: 20 strawberries

Storage: Store covered at room temperature for up to 3 days.

Variations: ***Tuxedo Strawberries***

20 fresh srawberries, washed and dried
16 ounces white chocolate
16 ounces bittersweet chocolate

1. Line a baking sheet with parchment or wax paper. Make sure the strawberries are completely dry.

2. Melt and temper the white chocolate (page 17), or simply melt the chocolate.

3. Holding strawberries by the stem, dip them into the white chocolate one at a time, covering about three-quarters of each berry.

4. Allow excess chocolate to run off before placing each dipped strawberry on the baking sheet.

5. While the white chocolate is setting, melt and temper the bittersweet chocolate (page 17), or simply melt the chocolate.

6. When the white chocolate has set, dip strawberries into the bittersweet chocolate one side at a time, leaving a "V" of white chocolate in the center of the flat side to resemble a tuxedo.

7. Replace strawberries on the baking sheet to set. Dip a toothpick or wooden skewer in the bittersweet chocolate and carefully draw bow ties and buttons on the white chocolate portions.

22a–c. **DRIED APPLE AND PEAR CHIPS**

General
Description:

Crunchy dried apple and pear chips are much more than just dried fruit. Apples or pears cut in paper-thin slices and steeped in sweet sugar syrup are oven-dried to make some of the healthiest chips around. Despite their dainty appearance, fruit chips are fairly easy to make.

History:

These fruit chips are made with the same techniques used for fresh **candied fruit**. They were likely created by confectioners as a more visually appealing way to present dried fruit. Today, fruit chips are often used as adornments for desserts in fine restaurants.

Serving
Suggestions:

These chips can garnish desserts, especially creamy ones, such as ice cream or puddings, since they provide crunchy contrast. But they are also healthy and satisfying snacks on their own. Dip them in cinnamon or tempered chocolate for a truly elegant confection.

Candy-Making
Notes:

Apples and pears are the easiest to turn into chips because they are firm; softer fruits will not work as well. It is easiest to make wafer-thin fruit slices with a mandolin. If you don't have one, try to cut the slices as uniformly as possible so that they will bake evenly.

Recipe:　**2 cups sugar**
2 firm apples or 2 underripe pears

1. **Preheat oven to 225°F. Line a few baking sheets with parchment paper or silicone baking mats.**

2. **Combine sugar and 2 cups water in a saucepan and bring to a boil, making sure all the sugar has dissolved. Remove from heat and set aside.**

3. **Using a sharp chef's knife or a mandolin, slice the fruit into approximately 1/16-inch slices.**

4. **Soak the slices in the sugar syrup for about 10 minutes, until they are translucent.**

5. **Use tongs to move slices to baking sheets, making sure they lie perfectly flat.**

6. **Dry the slices in the oven for 50 minutes to 1 hour, rotating halfway through. The chips will be dry and crisp when done.**

7. **Remove from oven and place on wire racks to cool.**

Yield:　About 30 chips

Storage:　Store in an airtight container in a cool, dry place for up to 2 months.

Variation: ***Chocolate-Dipped Fruit Chips***
With the addition of tempered chocolate, these chips go from a simple snack to elegant confection. Melt and temper 1 1/2 pounds of bittersweet chocolate (page 17). Dip each fruit chip halfway into the tempered chocolate, and place on a baking sheet lined with wax paper to set, about 1 hour.

23a–b. 📷   **FRUIT JELLIES**

General
Description:
These wiggly, jiggly jelly candies are tart, sweet, and made with real fruit juice. The use of gelatin to make colorful, fruit-flavored confections began with the invention of Jell-O, and family parties and restaurant buffets haven't been the same since. Jell-O is already flavored, but it is easy to use unflavored gelatin and fruit juice to make fresh fruit jellies at home.

History:
The use of gelatin for sweet dishes became popular in the Victorian era, when gelatin was sold in individual sheets. Today it is still sold in sheet form in Europe and in professional culinary supply stores worldwide. Powdered gelatin was invented in America in 1845. In the late-1880s, Pearle Wait and his wife added fruit flavoring to gelatin powder and christened it *Jell-O*. They sold their confection to Orator Woodward, who founded the Jell-O Company in 1923. Meanwhile, plain powdered gelatin was sold by the Knox Company

as an all-purpose product. It is the most popular brand of unflavored gelatin to this day.

Serving
Suggestions:

Make rainbow jellies by pouring a layer of jelly mixture into a baking pan, then pouring a different-colored layer on top after the first has set. Or add chopped fruit to the jelly mixture before it sets.

Candy-Making
Notes:

Almost any clear fruit juice can be used to make fruit jellies. Avoid using fresh tropical fruits such as pineapples, papayas, mangoes, or kiwis; they contain an enzyme that prevents the gelatin from setting properly. But canned tropical fruits will work because the heat involved in the canning process kills the enzyme.

Recipe:

4 tablespoons unflavored gelatin
4 cups clear fruit juice, such as cranberry,
strawberry, or blueberry
¹/₄ cup sugar
Few drops food coloring, if desired

1. **Set aside a 6-by-6-inch baking pan, molds, or dessert glasses of your choice.**

2. **Combine the gelatin with 1 cup of the fruit juice and let dissolve for about 5 minutes.**

3. **Combine remaining the fruit juice and sugar in a saucepan and cook over medium heat, stirring**

occasionally, until the sugar dissolves.

 4.   Add in the gelatin and stir until it dissolves fully
into the mixture. Add food coloring if desired.

5.   Pour mixture into pan, molds, or dessert glasses.
Refrigerate until it has fully set before serving.
Cut into cubes if desired.

Yield: About 20 cubes

Storage: Refrigerate in an airtight container for up to 1 week.

Variation: ***Champagne Jellies***
Replacing the fruit juice with Champagne creates an
elegant version perfect for hors d'oeuvres or dessert.
Substitute the fruit juice with Champagne or sparkling
wine. Create a simple summer dessert by layering
cubes of Champagne jelly in glasses with fresh berries.

24a–b.   **GUMDROPS**

General
Description: *Gumdrops are small, very chewy, jellylike candies that
come in a rainbow of colors and flavors.* They are
typically rounded on one end like a thimble and
rolled in granulated sugar for a sparkling appearance.
Gumdrops come in a variety of fruit flavors; sometimes they are spiced and called *spice drops*.

| History: | The origins of gumdrops are unclear; they appear to be another variant of gelatin-based candies that have remained popular over the years because of their distinctive shape and useful decorative properties. In the 1940s, one popular recipe among American housewives was gumdrop cake, which featured gumdrops baked into a spiced cake. Baskin-Robbins once had an ice cream flavor named Goody Goody Gumdrop, which featured gumdrops mixed into a tutti-frutti ice cream. However, the gumdrops froze too hard in the ice cream, and the company dropped the flavor. In America, February 15 is National Gumdrop Day. |

| Serving Suggestions: | Gumdrops can be eaten out of the hand, but they are also popularly used as decorations for gingerbread houses at Christmastime. |

| Candy-Making Notes: | Candy molds can be used instead of a baking pan. You can substitute fruit pectin for the gelatin. |

| Recipe: | **5 tablespoons unflavored gelatin**
$1/4$ cup sugar
1 tablespoon lemon juice
1 teaspoon vanilla or other fruit-flavored extract
Few drops food coloring, if desired
Granulated or sparkling sugar for rolling |

1. Line an 8-by-8-inch baking pan with a piece of foil long enough to hang over the edges and act as handles. Grease foil with cooking spray.

2. Combine the gelatin, sugar, and ¹/₂ cup water in a saucepan.

3. Cook over medium heat, stirring occasionally, until the sugar and gelatin dissolve.

4. Stir in the lemon juice and vanilla extract.

5. Pour the mixture into the prepared pan. Let set overnight until firm.

6. Use mini cookie cutters or a knife heated under hot water to cut the gumdrops into squares or other shapes. Roll in sugar.

Yield: About 60 gumdrops

Storage: Store in an airtight container for up to 1 week.

Variations: **Sour Gumdrops**
After you cut the gumdrops into shapes in step 6, roll them in **sherbet powder** (page 153) for tangy, sour gummy snacks.

Gumdrop Critters

Cut gumdrops with kitchen shears to create sticky surfaces for joining them together. Use a toothpick to make indentations, then insert sprinkles as eyes and noses.

25. **GUMMY BEARS**

General Description:

These fruit-flavored, chewy candies shaped like adorable teddy bears launched a trend of molded gummy candy. Typically made with gelatin, gummy bears (or *gummi bears*) have a firm, almost rubbery texture and come in a rainbow of colors corresponding with their flavors. The original maker of gummy bears, Haribo, still sells them around the world. With bear-shaped candy molds, you can make your own at home.

History:

Hans Riegel invented gummy bears in Bonn, Germany in 1922. Originally he called them *dancing bears*, but later changed them to *gummibarachen*, meaning "small rubber bears." The candy was a huge success, and his candy company, Haribo (an acronym for Hans Riegel Bonn), began selling the treats in North America in the 1980s. These little candies also inspired a 1985 Disney cartoon series: *The Adventures of the Gummi Bears*.

Serving
Suggestions:

Gummy bears traditionally come in cherry, orange, lemon, lime, and pineapple flavors, but you can use your favorite flavors and colors for homemade gummy bears.

Candy-Making
Notes:

You can substitute vegetarian fruit pectin for the gelatin. Any flavoring can be used.

Recipe:

6 tablespoons unflavored gelatin
$1/4$ cup sugar
Few drops cherry flavoring
Few drops food coloring

1. **Set aside clean, dry gummy-bear molds.**

2. **Combine the gelatin, sugar, and $1/3$ cup water in a saucepan.**

3. **Cook over medium heat, stirring occasionally, until the sugar and gelatin dissolve.**

4. **Add flavoring and food coloring and stir to combine.**

5. **Pour mixture into the molds. Refrigerate until it has fully set before removing.**

Yield: About 60 gummy bears

Storage: Store in an airtight container for up to 1 week.

26a–b.   **GUMMY WORMS**

General
Description:

These wriggly, worm-shaped candies are part of the candy-making tradition of imitating other objects. Brightly covered gummy worms are also one of the many foodstuffs often beloved by children but loathed by their parents. Gummy worms are usually made from gelatin, which gives them their chewiness and rubbery, surprisingly wormlike quality.

History:

Gummy worms are a variant of **gummy bears**. They were first made by Trolli, a German candy maker inspired by Haribo's gummy bears. Trolli capitalized on the success of gummy worms by extending their line of gummy shapes to include other insects, animals, and even foods. In the United States, July 15 is Gummy Worm Day.

Serving
Suggestions:

Kids will delight in these candies at Halloween. You can use gummy worms to decorate spooky cakes and cupcakes.

Candy-Making
Notes:

If you can find worm-shaped molds, pour the mixture into the molds instead of the pan in step 5. This recipe allows you to make gummy worms without a special mold.

Recipe:

12 tablespoons unflavored gelatin, divided in two
$^{1}/_{2}$ cup sugar, divided in two

Few drops cherry flavoring, or other flavoring
Few drops food coloring

1. **Set aside a 5-by-9-inch loaf pan.**

2. **Combine 6 tablespoons gelatin, $^1/_4$ cup sugar, and $^1/_3$ cup water in a saucepan.**

3. **Cook over medium heat until the mixture comes to a boil and the gelatin and sugar have dissolved.**

4. **Stir in flavoring and food coloring.**

5. **Pour mixture into the pan. Refrigerate until firm.**

6. **Repeat the process with a different flavor and coloring. Pour the mixture on top of the first layer of gelatin and refrigerate until firm.**

7. **Use a sharp knife to cut into thin, multicolored gummy worms.**

Yield: About 20 gummy worms

Storage: Store in an airtight container for up to 1 week.

Variation: *Sour Gummy Worms*
Roll worms in **sherbet powder** (page 153) for tangy, sour gummy snacks.

27. **LICORICE CHEWS**

General Description:

Licorice is an inky black, anise-flavored candy that inspires devotion or distaste. In North America, licorice candies are usually long, rubbery, chewy ropes. Red versions exist, but red licorice is a misnomer: The candy is typically fruit-flavored and contains no licorice flavor. In England, licorice is best known as a mix of small, hard candies called *liquorice allsorts*. People tend to eagerly seek out licorice or avoid it altogether; some even sort out black licorice jellybeans either to savor or to throw in the trash.

History:

The extract from the root of the licorice plant has been used since ancient times for flavoring and for medicinal purposes. The first licorice candies were made in the 1500s in Pontefract, England, where small soft disks of licorice extract mixed with sugar and gum arabic became known as *Pontefract cakes*. The licorice ropes so popular today in North America were invented in 1924 by the American Licorice Company. In the United States, April 12 is National Licorice Day.

Serving Suggestions:

Wrap these licorice candies in colorful wax papers and place them in the candy bowl, along with **caramels** and **taffy**. Offer licorice candies to trick-or-treaters at your own risk.

Candy-Making
Notes:

Although most licorice candy recipes still call for licorice extract, the flavor is often augmented by anise or other herbs and spices that have a similar taste. Anise oil is available at most grocery stores, and it tastes remarkably similar to licorice. Use a candy mold instead of a baking pan if desired.

Recipe:

1 cup sugar
1 cup heavy cream
¼ cup light corn syrup
1 tablespoon unsalted butter
⅛ teaspoon salt
1 teaspoon anise oil
A few drops of black paste food coloring

 1. **Line an 8-by-8-inch baking pan with a piece of parchment paper long enough to hang over the edges. Butter the parchment well.**

2. **Combine sugar and cream in a saucepan. Bring to a boil over medium-high heat, stirring constantly.**

 3. **Add corn syrup and continue cooking, stirring constantly until the temperature reaches 230°F.**

 4. **Add butter and stir to combine. Continue cooking mixture until it reaches 245°F.**

5. **Remove from heat and stir in salt, anise oil, and food coloring.**

 6. **Pour mixture into prepared pan and let cool.**

 7. **Remove licorice block from the pan and cut into squares or other shapes using a sharp, well-oiled knife. Wrap individual candies in wax papers to prevent them from losing their shape or sticking to each other.**

Yield: About 60 candies

Storage: Store in an airtight container for up to 1 week.

28. **MARRONS GLACÉS**

General Description: *These classic French Christmas sweetmeats are chestnuts candied over a period of several days and glazed to an alluring sheen.* Traditionally only the finest, largest chestnuts are used. Although the classic method of creating marrons glacés requires an intensive week-long candying process, this recipe reduces the candying time and still produces delicious results.

History: Chestnuts were first harvested in ancient Europe in the kingdom of Lydia, today part of Turkey. Travelers brought them to the rest of the Mediterranean, and the

Romans planted chestnut trees across Europe. Candied chestnuts were first made in Italy in the 15th century, but France claims to have perfected the complicated glacé technique in the 17th century, during the reign of Louis XIV. *Marron* is the French word for chestnut.

Serving Suggestions:

Marrons glacés are traditionally served at Christmastime in decorative paper cups. They are often used to decorate cakes.

Candy-Making Notes:

Try to find the largest, best-quality chestnuts. If you buy them skinned, you can skip steps 1 and 2 below. When candying chestnuts, some may become soft and fall apart; they are still delicious and don't need to be discarded. Puree broken marrons glacés with vanilla and sugar to make *crème de marrons*, a sweet spread.

Recipe:

1 pound chestnuts, shelled
2 cups sugar
1 tablespoon vanilla extract

 1. **Place chestnuts in a pot and cover with water.**

 2. **Bring to a boil over high heat and continue to boil for about 8 minutes.**

3. **Remove chestnuts and peel off skins; it is easiest while the nuts are still hot.**

4. In a clean pot, combine sugar, 1 cup water, and vanilla extract, and bring to a boil.

5. Drop in chestnuts and cook over medium-low heat for about 10 minutes.

6. Remove pot from heat, cover, and let nuts steep overnight.

7. The next day, bring mixture to a boil and let nuts cook for 1 minute; then remove from heat and let steep overnight again.

8. Repeat the process twice more.

9. Preheat oven to about 150°F. Line a baking sheet with parchment paper.

10. Drain nuts and place on the baking sheet.

11. Dry nuts in the oven for 2 hours or until fully dry.

Yield: About 20 chestnuts

Storage: Wrap individually in plastic and store in an airtight container for up to 1 week.

29. **PÂTES DE FRUITS**

General
Description:
These classic French confections are beautiful, jewel-like candies that taste like the pure essence of fruit. Pâtes de fruits look like sophisticated **fruit jellies**, but they are actually more like a concentrated, intense jam. They are made with pureed fruit cooked with pectin, which gives them a rich, pure fruit flavor and a denser, chewier consistency than gelatin-based jellies. Pâtes de fruits are usually cut into square pieces and covered in sugar for a sparkling appearance. The very best pâtes de fruits in France are prized for the quality of the ingredients and sold in high-end confectioneries alongside truffles and other chocolates.

History:
The ancient Greeks learned that cooking fruits with honey preserves them, thanks to naturally occurring fruit pectin. Auvergne, France, is credited with inventing the first pâtes de fruits in the 16th century. Today this city is still famous for the quality of its confections.

Serving
Suggestions:
Pâtes de fruits are traditional petits fours in fine restaurants. You can serve them with truffles after dinner.

Candy-Making
Notes:
The proportions of fruit, sugar, and pectin are key to ensuring that the mixture sets properly. If you want

to use other fruits, you may need to experiment and adjust the amounts to achieve the perfect consistency.

Recipe: **1 cup raspberries**
1½ teaspoons apple pectin
2½ tablespoons plus 1½ cups sugar
¼ cup corn syrup
1¼ teaspoons tartaric acid

1. **Coat an 8-by-8-inch baking pan with cooking spray and set aside.**

2. **Puree the raspberries in a food processor until smooth. Strain into a saucepan and cook over high heat until it begins to simmer.**

3. **Combine the apple pectin and 2½ tablespoons sugar. Add to the raspberry mixture and cook until it reaches a boil.**

4. **Add the remaining sugar and corn syrup, and cook mixture until it reaches 225°F.**

5. **Remove from heat and stir in tartaric acid. Let it cool.**

6. **Run the blade of a knife all around the edges to help loosen it from the pan. Cut pâtes de fruits into 1-inch squares and roll in sugar to coat.**

Yield:	About 60 candies
Storage:	Store in an airtight container for up to 1 week.

30. STUFFED DATES

General
Description:
These simple candies make one of the sweetest fruits even more delectable. Dates stuffed with fillings—savory or sweet—are a common dish in the Middle East and northern Africa. One of the most popular fillings is *marzipan*; the nutty paste complements the intense honeyed sweetness of the date. In Algeria the marizpan is often tinted green. These little sweetmeats are enjoyed as a healthy snack, elegant hors d'oeuvre, or simple dessert.

History:
The date palm is one of the most ancient plants on earth, and one of humanity's first sources of food. It originated in the Middle East and has played an essential role in the region's history and culture; dates are mentioned numerous times in the Quran and are traditionally eaten by Muslims to break their fast during the month of Ramadan. The ancient Arabs introduced the date palm to northern Africa and southeast Asia, where dates have become an integral part of the cuisine. They are also commonly served at Jewish holidays.

Serving
Suggestions:

This is an easy way to use your homemade **marzipan**, but store-bought marzipan works just as well. Serve stuffed dates as hors d'oeuvres or a sweet ending to an exotic meal.

Candy-Making
Notes:

Dates have high natural sugar content. However, their textures and flavors vary; experiment to find your favorite. Medjool dates are commonly found in North America. Large, plump fruits are easier to stuff.

Recipe:

10 ounces marzipan
2 tablespoons confectioners' sugar
1 teaspoon Grand Marnier or orange extract
12 large dates

1. **Combine marzipan, confectioners' sugar, and Grand Marnier in a food processor.**

2. **Slit the dates lengthwise, cutting nearly but not all the way through each date. Remove the pits.**

3. **Pinch off pieces of the marzipan mixture and form into 1¹/₂-inch logs. Press the logs into the dates, letting the filling show at the top.**

Yield: 12 dates

Storage: Store in an airtight container for up to 1 week. Marzipan and dates can keep for weeks if stored separately.

31. 📷 **SUGARPLUMS**

General
Description:

When visions of sugarplums dance in children's heads, it would be interesting to know exactly what sugarplums they dream of. Historically, the term *sugarplum* has referred to a wide variety of candies; the most recent confections to hold this name are soft, sticky balls of dried fruits and nuts, often rolled in shredded coconut or confectioners' sugar. They do not necessarily contain plums. Sometimes these candies are known as *fruit-and-nut balls*.

History:

The word *sugarplum* was first recorded in 1668 and used to describe small, oval, sugar-coated seeds. It may have been a general term for sugar-coated nuts or fruits that eventually evolved into **candied fruit** and **dragées**. Sugarplums were immortalized in Clement Clarke Moore's poem "A Visit from St. Nicolas" and Tchaikovsky's Sugar Plum Fairy in the *Nutcracker* ballet. Because of these popular influences, sugarplums have become indelibly linked to Christmas.

Serving
Suggestions:

Presented in gold foil cups, sugarplums are a crowd-pleaser at any Christmas table. You can roll them in a variety of toppings, from coconut to cocoa powder to confectioners' sugar.

Candy-Making
Notes:

You can substitute the fruits and nuts in this recipe. Dried cherries, figs, or raisins work well, as would hazelnuts, pistachios, or pecans. Try adding chopped **candied ginger** or **candied citrus peel**.

Recipe:
- **2 cups almonds, toasted and roughly chopped**
- **1 cup dried apricots**
- **1 cup pitted dates**
- **1 teaspoon ground cinnamon**
- **2 teaspoons grated orange zest**
- **2 tablespoons orange juice**
- **1 tablespoon honey**
- **Unsweetened flaked coconut for rolling**

1. **Line a baking sheet with parchment or wax paper.**

2. **Combine almonds, apricots, dates, cinnamon, and orange zest in a food processor and process into a finely ground mixture.**

3. **Add orange juice and honey, and combine until the mixture becomes a sticky ball.**

4. **Pinch off pieces of the mixture and form into 1-inch balls. Roll in coconut. Place on the baking sheet for about 1 hour until firm.**

Yield: About 30 sugarplums

Storage: Refrigerate in an airtight container between layers of wax paper for up to 1 week.

32. **TURKISH DELIGHT**

General
Description:

Small, jellylike cubes of Turkish delight are usually pink and taste of rosewater. In Turkey they are known as *rahat lokum* or *lokum,* which may be derived from *luqma(t),* the Arabic word for "morsel." In Greece they are known as *loukemiain.* Turkish delight is often dusted with confectioners' sugar to prevent sticking, further adding to its sweet, delicate flavor. It can be found in many colors and flavors—lemon, mint, bergamot, or cinnamon—and it may be covered in chocolate or studded with nuts, usually hazelnut, walnut, or pistachio.

History:

Since the 1400s, Turkish Delight has been sold at the Spice Bazaar in Istanbul, where stacks of candy are piled high on market tables. In the early 1800s British travelers brought it back to England, where it was first known as "lumps of delight" and later as "Turkish delight." In C. S. Lewis's *The Lion, The Witch, and The Wardrobe,* the White Witch lures Edmund Pevensie to her castle with promises of "whole rooms full of Turkish delight."

Serving
Suggestions:

At the end of a meal, serve a few pieces with a cup of coffee or tea. Or stack Turkish delight on trays for a party or Christmas gathering. Experiment with flavors like lemon or orange flower.

Candy-Making Notes:
Authentic Turkish delight is unlike most jelly-like candies because it does not contain gelatin or pectin; the only binder is the cornstarch. As a result, Turkish delight does not keep very long.

Recipe:
4 cups sugar
1 tablespoon lemon juice
1 teaspoon cream of tartar
1 cup plus ¹/₂ cup cornstarch
2 tablespoons rosewater
Red food coloring, if desired
¹/₂ cup confectioners' sugar

1. **Line an 8-by-8-inch baking pan with parchment paper and coat with cooking spray.**

2. **Combine sugar, 1¹/₂ cups water, and lemon juice in saucepan. Boil over medium heat until the mixture reaches 240°F, soft ball stage. Remove from heat.**

3. **Combine cream of tartar, 1 cup corn starch, and 2¹/₂ cups water in another saucepan and bring to a boil over medium heat. The mixture will become a very smooth, thick paste.**

4. **Slowly add the sugar mixture to the cornstarch mixture, whisking to combine. Reduce heat to low and simmer for 1 hour, stirring often.**

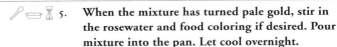

5. When the mixture has turned pale gold, stir in the rosewater and food coloring if desired. Pour mixture into the pan. Let cool overnight.

6. When you are ready to cut the Turkish delight, sift confectioners' sugar and ¹/₂ cup cornstarch in a bowl.

7. Turn out Turkish delight onto a clean surface. Using a sharp, oiled knife, cut into 1-inch pieces.

8. Toss pieces in confectioners' sugar mixture.

Yield: About 60 pieces

Storage: Serve immediately or store in airtight container between layers of wax paper for up to 3 days.

Sugary Sweet

33.   **ACID DROPS**

General
Description:

*These shiny, brilliantly colored candies are a cornerstone
of British confectionery, or* boiled sweets, *as the British
call them.* They have a light tangy flavor from the
added citric acid, but many variations of colors and
flavors exist. Some of the most popular are fruit drops,
especially *pear drops*, which are colored yellow and
purple, and *barley sugars*, which are flavored with barley. The French make versions of these drop candies
that are flavored with fruit juices or floral essences.

History:

Clear drop candies were one of the first candies made
by boiling sugar. British confectioners learned that
adding acids such as lemon juice or cream of tartar to
cooking syrup keeps sugar from crystallizing, hence
the name *acid drops*. Originally, drop candies were
formed by cutting the hot candy mixture into drops;
in the mid-1800s, machines automated the process
and molded the candies into various shapes and
embossed designs.

Serving
Suggestions:

Substitute other flavors for the lemon extract to make
a variety of acid drops. You can also color the drops
to coordinate with the color scheme of a wedding or
dinner party. Serve them in candy bowls at afternoon
tea or as after-dinner sweets.

| Candy-Making Notes: | Candy-flavoring extracts or oils are the best for hard candy, but regular extracts from your supermarket will work. Wait until the mixture has cooled slightly before adding them so that they do not evaporate in the heat. Be extremely careful when working the hot candy mixture. Use lozenge molds if desired. |

Recipe: ***Lemon Drops***

1 cup sugar
¹/₂ teaspoon cream of tartar
2 teaspoons citric acid (crystals or powdered)
¹/₂ teaspoon lemon extract
Few drops yellow food coloring
Confectioners' sugar for rolling

1. **Coat a large baking pan or marble slab with cooking spray. Lightly spray a pair of kitchen shears.**

2. **Combine sugar, cream of tartar, and ¹/₂ cup water in a saucepan. Bring to a boil over medium-high heat.**

3. **Continue cooking until the mixture reaches 300°F, hard crack stage. Immediately remove saucepan from heat.**

4. **Pour candy onto the baking pan or marble slab. Sprinkle the citric acid, lemon extract, and food coloring over the candy.**

5. Using a bench scraper or metal spatula, turn the mass in on itself until the citric acid and coloring have been distributed evenly.

⧗ 6. Let the candy rest until it is cool enough to handle, but do not let it harden completely.

✂ ▭ 7. Roll the candy into long ropes. Cut the ropes into small pieces and roll them in the confectioners' sugar to coat before letting them fully harden on a clean baking sheet.

Yield: About 50 pieces

▭ Storage: Store in an airtight container for up to 3 months.

Variation: **Sour Lemon Drops**
For extra sour lemon candy, roll the drops in **sherbet powder** instead of confectioners' sugar.

---

34. 📷 **BUTTERSCOTCH DROPS**

General Description: *Golden, soft butterscotch drops are a cross between caramels and toffee drops.* They are made with nearly the same ingredients as **English toffee**, but the mixture is cooked to 270°F, or soft crack, which results in a softer, chewier candy. Butterscotch has become known as a flavor, similar to caramel. The two flavors are commonly confused, but butterscotch, unlike caramel, derives its rich, deep flavor from brown sugar.

History:

It is likely that the name *butterscotch* comes from the word *scotch*, which meant "to cut or score" in the early 1800s, when butterscotch was invented. Butterscotch candy was scored while it was still cooling so that it could be broken into pieces when hard. Early butterscotch recipes called for white granulated sugar, but today most use brown sugar to achieve the desired flavor.

Serving Suggestions:

Wrap butterscotch candies in foil or wax paper and place in the candy dish along with other old-fashioned favorites, such as **English toffee**.

Candy-Making Notes:

Instead of pouring the whole mixture into a pan and scoring it into pieces, you can pour it into molds or drop spoonfuls of the hot butterscotch onto sheets; they will form flat, round drops.

Recipe:

1 cup light brown sugar
1 cup sugar
2 teaspoons white vinegar
1 pinch salt
¼ cup unsalted butter
½ teaspoon vanilla extract

1. **Line an 11-by-17-inch baking sheet with foil and**

grease well, or line with a silicone baking mat.

2. **Combine the sugars, ¹/₂ cup water, vinegar, and salt in a saucepan. Bring to a boil over medium-high heat.**

3. **When the temperature of the mixture reaches 230°F, add the butter and carefully stir to combine.**

4. **Continue cooking mixture until it reaches 270°F.**

5. **Remove from heat immediately and stir in vanilla.**

6. **Pour mixture onto the baking sheet. Let it cool slightly before using a sharp knife to score into squares.**

7. **Let cool completely before breaking into pieces.**

Yield: About 60 pieces

Storage: Store in an airtight container for up to 1 week.

35. **CANDY CANES**

General Description: *These peppermint-flavored, brilliantly striped candies are hung on Christmas trees, tucked into stockings, and tied to presents.* Candy canes are made of layers of variously colored hard candy rolled together and formed into a curved shape. They are usually red and white, although other color combinations can be found. Candy canes are most prevalent in North America and Europe during the holiday season.

History: Several interesting stories surround the creation of candy canes. The most plausible say that in 1670 a choirmaster of the Cologne Cathedral in Germany handed out sugar candy to the children in his choir to keep them quiet during the Christmas service. He curved the sugar sticks into the shape of a shepherd's crook in honor of the holiday; the practice then spread throughout Europe and to colonial America. Originally, candy canes were pure white. The distinctive red and white striping and peppermint flavor were added in the early 1900s.

Serving Suggestions: Candy canes are the quintessential Christmas decoration, especially when they are handmade. Crushed candy canes can be used like **peppermints** in other desserts: Sprinkle them over ice cream or on top of cakes and cookies. Along with **gumdrops** and **chocolate bars**, candy canes commonly decorate gingerbread houses.

Candy-Making Notes: Twisting hot sugar is something best left to commercial candy makers. This recipe for old-fashioned

candy canes is easily made at home since the dough
is easy to twist at room temperature.

Candy Cane Twists

$^1/_2$ cup unsalted butter, room temperature
1 tablespoon heavy cream
$3^1/_2$ to $4^1/_2$ cups confectioners' sugar
$^1/_4$ teaspoon peppermint extract or 1 drop
    peppermint oil
Few drops red food coloring
1 to 2 tablespoons corn syrup

1. Line a baking sheet with parchment paper.

2. In a stand mixer with the paddle attachment, beat
the butter and cream until smooth.

3. Add confectioners' sugar 1 cup at a time, and beat
until it forms a smooth dough. Add the peppermint extract and beat to combine.

4. Divide the dough into two portions. Add red food
coloring to one portion.

5. If the dough seems too firm, add 1 to 2 tablespoons of corn syrup to keep it pliable.

6. **Pinch off pieces of dough from each portion and roll them into long ropes about ¹/₂-inch thick. Layer a red piece on top of a white piece and twist together a few times to create a striped effect.**

7. **Trim the ropes to desired length. Place on the baking sheet to set overnight before serving.**

Yield: About 20 candy cane twists

Storage: Store in an airtight container in a cool, dry place for up to 1 week.

CANDY CORN

General Description: *These little triangular-shaped candies are colored in bands of yellow, orange, and white to mimic a ripe kernel of corn.* Candy corn is associated with Halloween in North America and makes its appearance in large quantities as the holiday approaches.

History: Candy corn was invented in the 1880s by George Renninger of the now defunct Wunderlee Candy Company. It was handmade from sugar syrup, fondant, and **marshmallows**. The manufacturing was taken over in 1900 by the Goelitz Candy Company, today known as the Jelly Belly Candy Company. In the United States, October 30 is National Candy Corn Day.

Serving
Suggestions:

Halloween wouldn't be complete without pumpkins and candy corn. Vary the colors for other holidays. You can make Indian corn (brown, orange, and white), reindeer corn (red, green, and white), and cupid corn (red, pink, and white). Candy corn traditionalists eat each stripe of color one nibble at a time.

Candy-Making
Notes:

When forming the ropes of dough into one piece, lightly running a rolling pin over the top will help press the colors together.

Recipe:

2 1/2 cups confectioners' sugar
1/4 cup dry powdered milk
1/4 teaspoon salt
1 cup sugar
2/3 cup corn syrup
1/3 cup unsalted butter
1 teaspoon vanilla extract
Food coloring, if desired

1. **Combine confectioners' sugar, powdered milk, and salt in a bowl and set aside.**

2. **Combine sugar, corn syrup, and butter in a saucepan. Bring to a boil over high heat, stirring constantly. Reduce heat to medium and cook for another 5 minutes, stirring occasionally.**

3. **Remove from heat and stir in vanilla extract.**

4. **Add the dry milk mixture to the saucepan, and stir to combine. Let mixture rest for a few minutes until it is cool enough to handle.**

5. **Divide dough into 3 equal parts and place each portion in a bowl. Add coloring as desired.**

6. **Knead each portion of dough until the coloring is evenly distributed and the dough is smooth and stiff.**

7. **Roll each portion into a rope about ¹/₂ inch thick.**

8. **Place the three ropes of dough next to each other to form a long rectangle. Use a rolling pin to gently press them together.**

9. **Using a sharp knife, cut the dough into triangles and place on a baking sheet. Let set for about 1 hour.**

Yield: About 80 pieces

Storage: Store in an airtight container in a cool, dry place for up to 2 months.

37. **CARAMELS**

General
Description:

Caramels are soft, golden brown, square or rectangular candies that taste like caramel—hence their name. It's easy to confuse this caramel candy with caramel: Caramel is sugar that has been cooked to about 320°F, melted, and caramelized until it is very hard and has a dark brown, glassy appearance. Caramel candy, by contrast, is sugar that has been cooked with glucose and dairy products, such as milk and butter, to about 245°F, or firm ball stage. The added ingredients and lower cooking temperature give the candy its softer, more pliable texture, and its caramel flavor comes from browning of the sugar and dairy. Caramels are usually wrapped because they become sticky.

History:

The caramelization of sugar was developed in France in the 17th century; however, caramel candies were invented in America in the 1880s. Milton Hershey of Hershey's Chocolates fame got his start making caramels. His first successful candy company was Lancaster Caramel Company in Pennsylvania.

Serving
Suggestions:

Wrap caramels in wax papers and serve them in a candy dish. Try dipping them in tempered chocolate. If you like salty-sweet flavors, try **fleur de sel caramels**.

Candy-Making
Notes:

Caramels are best made on a cool, dry day because humidity interferes with the candies setting up properly. If you find your caramels are too soft, they may be undercooked. You can always put the mixture into a saucepan and recook it to a higher temperature.

Recipe:

1 cup sugar
1 cup heavy cream
¼ cup light corn syrup
1 tablespoon unsalted butter
⅛ teaspoon salt
1 tablespoon vanilla extract

1. **Line an 8-by-8-inch baking pan with a piece of parchment paper long enough to hang over the edges. Butter the parchment well.**

2. **Combine the sugar and cream in a saucepan. Bring to a boil over medium-high heat, stirring constantly to prevent burning.**

3. **Add the corn syrup and continue cooking until the mixture reaches 230°F.**

4. **Add the butter and stir to combine. Continue cooking to 245°F.**

5. **Remove from heat and stir in salt and vanilla.**

6. **Pour mixture into prepared pan to cool and harden.**

7. **Remove the caramel block from the pan and cut into squares or other shapes using a sharp, well-oiled knife. Wrap caramels in wax papers.**

Yield: About 60 caramels

Storage: Store in an airtight container in a cool, dry place for up to 2 weeks.

38. **CRYSTALLIZED GINGER**

General Description: *Ginger root is candied in a sugar syrup using the same process as* **candied fruit**, *resulting in soft, slightly chewy slices or cubes of ginger dusted in more sugar for a sparkling appearance.* Because ginger—especially mature roots—can be too intense to eat raw, candying tones down the spiciness so that it can be enjoyed as a sweet.

History: Ginger originated in China and spread to India and Southeast Asia; it is still an essential part of Asian cuisines. Candied ginger was likely first made in Asia, where the root is revered for its healthful properties. In Europe and North America, ginger is more commonly found in powdered form and used in sweet recipes, such as gingerbread.

Serving
Suggestions:
❄ ✄

Crystallized ginger is a lovely Christmastime sweet; you can present the candies as they are or dipped in tempered chocolate. Diced fine, crystallized ginger is a wonderful addition to holiday recipes that call for ginger, such as fruitcake, gingerbread, sugarplums, and truffles.

Candy-Making
Notes:

Choose fresh, young ginger for this recipe: The roots should be firm and evenly colored. The sugar syrup that results from candying the ginger is an added bonus; you can save it to drizzle over poached fruit or ice cream or for use in recipes that call for sugar syrup.

Recipe:

8 ounces ginger (about 2 roots)
2 cups sugar, plus extra for coating

1. **Peel the ginger and cut into $^1/_8$-inch slices.**

2. **Combine the ginger slices and sugar in a saucepan and add enough water to just cover the mixture.**

3. **Bring mixture to a boil over medium-high heat. Lower the heat until it simmers steadily.**

4. **Let the mixture simmer for 3 hours, checking occasionally to make sure it does not boil or burn.**

5. **Once the ginger is tender and almost translucent and the syrup is thick, it has been candied. Remove**

the ginger pieces from the syrup and place them on a wire rack set over paper towels to finish draining overnight. Save syrup if desired.

6. **Toss the ginger slices in sugar to coat.**

Yield: About 1 cup crystallized ginger

Storage: Store in an airtight container at room temperature. Crystallized ginger will last almost indefinitely.

39. **DULCE DE LECHE**

General Description:
*The South American version of **caramels**, dulce de leche is a versatile sweet enjoyed as a syrup, spread, and candy.* Dulce de leche is made by cooking milk and sugar together until the mixture caramelizes into a thick pudding. Further cooking reduces it to a firm, chewy candy with a rich, butterscotch-like flavor.

History:
Dulce de leche means "milk sweet" in Spanish. It is believed to have been invented in South America. The Mexican version is called *cajeta* and often made with a mixture of cow's milk and goat's milk. In Peru and Chile, it is called *manjar blanco* and made with similar ingredients, but the milk and sugar are cooked slowly so that it does not turn brown.

Serving
Suggestions:
❄ ☀ ☁ ❄ ✂

The consistency of dulce de leche depends on how
long you cook the condensed milk. As a liquid sauce,
it can be spooned over ice cream or drizzled over
tarts. As a thicker jam, it can be spread over toast.
Packed into jars, dulce de leche makes a thoughtful
gift. And at its firmest, it can be cut into squares and
enjoyed as a candy.

Candy-Making
Notes:

Although dulce de leche can be made from scratch,
one of the easiest ways to make it is with a can of
sweetened condensed milk.

Recipes:

Easy Dulce de Leche

1 can (14 ounces) sweetened condensed milk

1. **Spray an 8-by-8-inch baking pan with cooking
spray.**

2. **Pour the condensed milk into a metal bowl over a
pot of simmering water.**

3. **Cook over low heat, stirring occasionally to prevent the bottom from burning.**

4. **Let the milk cook for 3¹/₂ hours until it is very
thick and dark golden.**

5. **Remove from heat and pour into the baking pan.**

Let cool overnight before cutting into 2-inch pieces or rolling into balls.

Yield: About 16 pieces

Storage: Refrigerate in an airtight container for up to 1 week.

40.   **ENGLISH TOFFEE**

General Description: *English toffee is an old-fashioned hard toffee that comes in lozenge-shaped drops or large slabs.* Traditionally, the toffee slabs were so hard that a hammer was necessary to break them into pieces; today, some English toffee is still sold with a little hammer as a novelty. Toffees in drop form are most popular in Britain; they are flavored with treacle, licorice, or nuts and sold wrapped in colorful foils. *See also* **almond buttercrunch** and **butterscotch drops**.

History: The history of hard toffee is intertwined with that of chewy taffy in the United Kingdom: Both candies were originally made with molasses and evolved from similar recipes. The word *toffee* may have come from *tafia*, a West Indian rum made from molasses. Walkers' Nonsuch, one of the oldest makers of toffees in England, still sells a variety of toffees, from drops to sticks to slabs.

Serving
Suggestions:

Unlike **caramels**, toffees are often flavored with other ingredients, so you can try adding different extracts or chopped nuts. Brazil nuts are a very popular addition. Wrap toffees in brightly colored foil.

Candy-Making
Notes:

If you want to make drops, you can pour the mixture into molds in step 5.

Recipe:

1 cup sugar
¹/₃ cup light brown sugar
1 tablespoon light corn syrup
¹/₄ cup unsalted butter, cut into pieces
¹/₈ teaspoon salt
³/₄ teaspoon vanilla extract

1. **Line an 11-by-17-inch baking pan with foil and grease well, or line with a silicone baking mat.**

2. **Combine sugars, corn syrup, 2 tablespoons water, butter, and salt in a saucepan. Cook over medium heat, stirring until it comes to a boil.**

3. **Continue cooking without stirring until the mixture reaches 298°F, hard crack stage.**

4. **Remove from heat and stir in vanilla.**

5. **Pour mixture into baking pan. Let it cool slightly before using a sharp knife to score into squares.**

6. **Let cool completely before breaking into pieces.**

Yield: About 60 pieces

Storage: Store in an airtight container for up to 1 week.

 ## FLEUR DE SEL CARAMELS

General Description:
: *Fleur de sel adds a burst of salty flavor to sweet* caramels. It has become a popular addition in recent years: The large crystals give a distinct crunch to the candy, and the tang of the salt is a wonderful contrast to the caramels' smooth sweetness.

History:
: Salted butter caramels have long been a regional favorite in Brittany, France, where fleur de sel is harvested from the sea. In the 1990s, French pastry chef Pierre Hermé popularized chocolates salted with fleur de sel; he then launched a trend with the invention of his famous salted caramel macaron.

Serving Suggestions:
: Wrapped in wax papers, fleur de sel caramels make a beautiful presentation in the candy dish. Take these salty-sweet confections one step further and dip them in tempered chocolate.

Candy-Making Notes:	Caramels are best made on a cool, dry day because humidity prevents them from setting up properly. Watch the cooking sugar carefully to prevent burning.

Recipe:
1 cup sugar
1 cup heavy cream
$^1/_4$ cup light corn syrup
1 tablespoon unsalted butter
$^1/_2$ teaspoon fleur de sel
1 tablespoon vanilla extract

1. **Line an 8-by-8-inch baking pan with a piece of parchment paper long enough to hang over the edges. Butter the parchment well.**

2. **Combine the sugar and cream in a saucepan. Bring to a boil over medium-high heat, stirring constantly to prevent burning.**

3. **Add the corn syrup and continue cooking until the mixture reaches 230°F.**

4. **Add the butter and stir carefully to combine. Continue cooking mixture until it reaches 245°F.**

5. **Remove from heat, and stir in salt and vanilla.**

6. **Pour mixture into pan to cool and harden.**

7. **Remove the caramel block from the pan and cut into squares using a sharp, well-oiled knife.**

8. **Sprinkle a few grains of fleur de sel on top of the cut caramels before wrapping.**

Yield: About 60 caramels

Storage: Store in an airtight container in a cool, dry place for up to 1 week.

Variation: ***Fleur de Sel Caramels Dipped in Dark Chocolate***
One of U.S. president Barack Obama's favorite candies is a salted caramel covered in dark chocolate from Fran's Chocolates in Seattle, Washington. To make your own, dip the cut caramels in tempered dark chocolate (page 17). Top with a few grains of fleur de sel.

42. **HARD CANDY**

General Description: *Hard candy is one of the oldest and simplest forms of sugar candy: It comes in a variety of beautiful forms, from **lemon drops** to **candy canes**.* In confectioner's terms, *hard candy* refers to a hot sugar syrup with no fats added, which is pulled and stretched like taffy until it becomes opaque. The pulling action aerates and lightens the candy and gives it a glossy, satinlike finish. The British are masters of hard candy, and their sweet shops contain a dizzying array of these treats.

History:

Middle Easterners invented pulled hard candy and introduced this candy-making method to Europe, along with sugar itself, in the 7th and 8th centuries. The British took a fancy to hard candies. Today, some of the most common British hard candies are **humbugs**—pillow-shaped drops flavored with peppermint and striped black, brown, and yellow.

Serving Suggestions:

With their vibrant colors and shiny finish, hard candies are some of the prettiest sweets around. Experiment with different colors and flavors.

Candy-Making Notes:

A marble slab is a good surface for working candy because it helps the candy cool quickly. Be extremely careful when working with the hot candy mixture. Wearing latex gloves helps. If the candy becomes too hard to manipulate, place it on a baking sheet in a 200°F oven for a minute. If you don't want to pull the candy, pour it into molds after step 3.

Recipe:

3 cups sugar
1 cup light corn syrup
½ tsp peppermint extract or other flavoring extract
Food coloring, if desired

1. **Coat a marble slab or baking sheet with cooking spray. Lightly spray a pair of kitchen shears.**

2. Combine sugar, corn syrup, and $1/4$ cup water in a saucepan. Bring to a boil over medium heat and continue cooking to 300°F, hard crack stage, without stirring.

3. Remove from heat and stir in peppermint extract and food coloring.

4. Pour candy onto the marble slab or baking sheet. Let it cool for 5 minutes, using a metal spatula to flip it so that it cools evenly.

5. When the candy has cooled enough to handle but is still hot, pull it with your hands, stretching and gathering until it becomes opaque and satiny.

6. Pull the candy into a long rope about $1/2$ inch thick. Cut candy into bite-size pieces using the shears. Place pieces on a cool baking sheet to cool.

7. When the pieces have fully cooled, wrap in cellophane.

Yield: About 60 candies

Storage: Store in an airtight container in a cool, dry place for up to 2 months.

43. **HONEY TAFFY**

General
Description:

This golden, chewy taffy captures the natural sweetness of honey. Its stiff, chewy texture comes from the taffy-making process: The candy is pulled over and over until it is dense and opaque. Then it is typically cut into small pieces and wrapped in wax paper to prevent sticking.

History:

In Valencia, Spain, Neolithic cave paintings show people gathering honey from a nest. The ancient Egyptians were one of the first civilizations to develop beekeeping, a practice that spread throughout Europe. Honey was valued for its medicinal properties, revered as an elixir of the gods, and prized as a sweetener. Before sugar became widely available in Asia and Europe, honey was the sweetener of choice in cooking and baking. Honey is still used as a natural alternative to white sugar.

Serving
Suggestions:

Try different honeys to find your favorite. The flavor of honey lightens when heated, so stronger, more robust types may work better than delicate ones. You can arrange honey taffy pieces in a pretty box with **caramels** for a distinctive holiday gift.

Candy-Making
Notes:

Pull the taffy mixture as much as possible; you may want to enlist helpers for some extra arm power. Wrap pieces of taffy in wax paper so they do not lose their shape.

Recipe:
1 cup sugar
¹/₂ cup honey
1 tablespoon unsalted butter
¹/₈ teaspoon salt
¹/₄ teaspoon vanilla extract

 1. Spray a large baking sheet or marble slab with cooking spray. Lightly spray a pair of kitchen shears. Set aside wax papers for wrapping the taffy pieces.

 2. Combine sugar, honey, 1 cup water, butter, and salt in a saucepan and stir to combine.

 3. Cook over medium heat, stirring until sugar is dissolved.

 4. Continue cooking to 265°F, hard ball stage, without stirring. Remove from heat.

 5. Add the vanilla extract and stir to combine.

 6. Turn out the mixture onto the baking sheet or marble slab, and let it cool to room temperature. Turn the mass over a few times so it cools evenly.

7. Butter hands lightly and pull taffy, stretching and gathering it until the mass becomes opaque and difficult to pull.

8. **Pull the taffy into a long rope about ¹/₂ inch thick. Cut into bite-size pieces using kitchen shears.**

 9. **Wrap each piece immediately in wax paper.**

Yield: About 50 pieces

Storage: Store in an airtight container for up to 1 month.

 HOREHOUND DROPS

General Description:
This old-fashioned remedy for sore throats is the predecessor to commercial cough drops. Made from the leaves of the horehound plant, this dark brown candy comes in small lozenge-shaped drops or straight sticks. Because of horehound's naturally bittersweet flavor, sugar is added to sweeten the taste. Horehound candy has a slightly herbal, menthol-like flavor, making it some of the sweetest medicine around.

History:
Horehound plants originated in Europe but are now found in many parts of the world. The ancient Greeks and Egyptians used the herb to treat a variety of ailments. Europeans brewed it into teas to treat coughs and colds. As the British art of boiled sugar candy developed, horehound was one of the flavorings commonly used. Horehound candy was also popular in colonial America.

Serving
Suggestions:
❇ ☀ ❀ ❄

Horehound can be a soothing, natural alternative to commercially made cough drops. You can also pour the hot horehound syrup into **lollipop** molds and create old-fashioned suckers; serve them with **salt-water taffy** and **candy canes** for a vintage candy shop experience.

Candy-Making
Notes:
⚠

There are two varieties of horehound, white and black; be sure you use white horehound. Dried horehound can be found at health food stores. As with all herbs and plants used for medicinal purposes, children and pregnant women should avoid consuming large amounts of horehound candy.

Recipe:

2 cups fresh horehound leaves or ¹/₂ cup dried white horehound

2 cups sugar

¹/₄ cup light corn syrup

⊞ 1. **Line a baking sheet with a piece of greased foil or a silicone baking mat. Or set aside a drop-candy mold.**

🍳🔥⏳ 2. **Combine the horehound with 1 cup water in a saucepan. Bring to a boil over high heat. Remove from heat let steep for 30 minutes.**

3. **Strain water into a clean saucepan. Add sugar and corn syrup and bring to a boil over medium-high heat.**

 4. **Continue cooking until the mixture reaches 298°F, hard crack stage.**

 5. **Pour the mixture into the baking sheet or drop candy mold. Let set about 2 hours before breaking into pieces.**

Yield: About 2 cups of horehound candy

 Storage: Store in an airtight container for up to 1 month.

---

45. 📷 **HUMBUGS**

General Description: *Not even Ebenezer Scrooge could say "Bah, humbug!" to these minty, pillow-shaped sweets made of pulled sugar.* Humbugs are English candy drops that are typically flavored with peppermint and striped in colors such as black and white, brown and cream, or green, brown, and yellow. Brightly colored fruit-flavored humbugs are a popular variation.

History: Today, humbugs are one of the most popular hard candies in the United Kingdom. They are also enjoyed in Canada and Australia. It is unclear how these sweets got their name. The word *humbug* means "deceptive nonsense" and was popularized by Ebenezer Scrooge in Charles Dickens's *A Christmas Carol*. In 2001, the Sela Confectionery made the largest humbug in the world: a 30-inch long, 70-pound mint humbug, but the giant sweet was stolen days before it was to be auctioned off for charity.

Serving
Suggestions:

Humbugs are thought to be cozy, "warming" candies, so they are eaten during the winter months. Wrap prettily striped humbugs in cellophane for a humorous Christmas gift.

Candy-Making
Notes:

A marble slab is a good work surface because it helps the candy cool quickly; if you don't have one, a baking sheet will do. Use extreme caution when working with the hot candy mixture. Wearing latex gloves helps. If the candy becomes too hard to manipulate, place it on a baking sheet in a 200°F oven for a minute.

Recipe:

3 cups sugar
1 cup light corn syrup
¼ cup water
½ teaspoon peppermint extract
Food coloring, if desired

1. **Coat a marble slab or large baking sheet with cooking spray. Lightly spray a pair of kitchen shears.**

2. **Combine sugar, corn syrup, and water in a sauce-pan. Bring to a boil over medium heat. Continue cooking without stirring until the candy reaches 300°F, hard crack stage.**

3. **Remove from heat and stir in peppermint extract and food coloring.**

4. **Pour candy onto the marble slab or baking sheet. Let it cool for about 5 minutes, using a bench scraper or metal spatula to occasionally turn the mass in on itself so that it cools evenly.**

5. **When the candy has cooled enough to handle but is still hot, begin pulling it with your hands, stretching and gathering it until it is opaque and satiny.**

6. **Pull the candy into a long rope about ¹/₂ inch thick. Cut it into bite-size pieces using the shears. Place pieces on a baking sheet to cool.**

7. **Wrap the cooled candies in cellophane.**

Yield: About 60 humbugs

Storage: Store in an airtight container in a cool, dry place for up to 2 months.

46a–b. 📷 **LOLLIPOPS**

General
Description:

What easier way to enjoy candy on the go than with a lollipop, the round, sugary hard candy on a stick? Lollipops are made of hot sugar syrup that is colored, flavored, and poured into molds lined with lollipop sticks. Novelty forms include spherical pops with chewy or liquid centers and those cast into unusual shapes, such as teddy bears or fruits.

History:

People have been using sticks to eat honey and other sweet concoctions since medieval times. The term *lollipop* originated in London in the 1780s, and at first it referred to any sweet; today some stickless sweets are still called *lollies* in Britain. The term did not travel to America until 1908, when George Smith patented the word for his line of hard candies on sticks. He claimed to have taken the name from his favorite racing horse, Lolly Pop. However, the word returned to public domain in 1931 and can be used to refer to any candy on a stick. Many candy companies claim to have invented the machine that automated the lollipop-making process; ironically, lollipops are one of the simplest candies to make at home.

Serving
Suggestions:
❄ ☀ ♧ ❄

Many beautiful and creatively shaped plastic molds can be used to make lollipops. If you don't have molds, simply pour or spoon the syrup onto a pan lined with parchment paper or a silicone baking mat, and place a stick into each drop of candy. Be sure to eat a lollipop on July 20, Lollipop Day in the United States.

Candy-Making Notes:

Candy-flavoring extracts or oils are the best agents for flavoring hard candy. If you cannot find them, use regular extracts from your supermarket. Be careful when working with the hot candy mixture.

Recipe:

1 cup sugar
¹/₃ cup light corn syrup
¹/₂ teaspoon cherry or other flavor extract
Few drops food coloring, if desired
Lollipop sticks

 1. **Combine sugar, corn syrup, and ¹/₂ cup water in a saucepan. Bring to a boil over medium-high heat.**

 2. **Continue cooking until the mixture reaches 300°F, hard crack stage. Remove from heat and cool to about 275°F.**

3. **Stir in the cherry flavoring and food coloring.**

 4. **Pour the mixture into the lollipop molds. Insert the sticks into the slots on the molds. Allow to cool and harden for 15 minutes before unmolding.**

Yield: About 10 lollipops

Storage: Wrap lollipops in cellophane that is twist-tied shut, and store them in a cool dry place for up to 1 month.

47. **MAPLE CANDY**

General
Description: *Maple candy in the shape of falling leaves is a tasty reminder of autumn.* Little more than maple syrup cooked down to its sugary essence, this candy has been made since the colonial days in North America. It is still a popular holiday gift from maple-producing areas in North America, such as Vermont, Wisconsin, and Quebec.

History: When British and French colonists settled the eastern coast of North America, Native Americans introduced them to a sweet syrup derived from the sap of the maple trees native to the region. It is not surprising that they soon used this cheap, local substitute for sugar to make a version of sugar candy. A common wintertime activity is making *Jack wax* or *sugar on snow*: pouring hot maple syrup on snow and eating the instantly frozen pieces.

Serving
Suggestions: This is the perfect recipe for candy molds in the shape of leaves, acorns, or other fall-themed objects. Boxes of homemade maple candy are a fitting autumn gift.

Candy-Making Notes:	Be sure to use real maple syrup, not imitation "maple-flavored" syrup. Maple syrup comes in several grades. In the United States, it comes in grades A and B, whereas in Canada it comes in grades #1 to #3. Grades A and #1 are the mildest and work best for a light, delicate candy. Use a higher grade if you want a stronger maple flavor.

Recipe: **2 cups maple syrup**
1 tablespoon unsalted butter

1. **Combine maple syrup and butter in a saucepan. Bring to a boil over medium heat. Watch carefully so the mixture does not boil over.**

2. **Continue cooking until it reaches 240°F, soft ball stage. Remove from heat and let cool for about 5 minutes.**

3. **Beat the mixture vigorously with a wooden spoon until it becomes very thick and creamy and loses its glossy sheen. Do not let the mixture set.**

4. **Immediately pour the mixture into candy molds to set, about 20 minutes.**

Yield: About 24 maple candies

Storage: Store in an airtight container between sheets of wax paper for up to 1 month.

48. **PASTELI**

General
Description: *Perhaps one of the first candies ever made, these Greek honey candies are thin, chewy bars of honey mixed with sesame seeds.* The most traditional version of this ancient Greek specialty uses just these two ingredients and is sweet and nutty, sticky, and crunchy. Other versions contain sugar or corn syrup, which create a firmer, crunchier bar. Sometimes nuts and dried fruit are added; pistachios are popular. With nutritious ingredients and no refined sugar, pasteli is one of the most healthful candies.

History: Honey is the world's first sweetener. The Greek islands, famed for their varieties of flowers, were early producers of honey. Ancient Greeks valued bees and the honey they produced. It is possible that ambrosia, the food of the Greek gods, was in fact honey. Homer's epic *Iliad* includes a reference to a sesame and honey pie, perhaps a forebearer of pasteli. Different varieties of pasteli exist throughout Greece, each using local honeys and ingredients to create a unique version of this ancient candy.

Serving
Suggestions:

Because both honey and sesame seeds are nutritious, these candies are a healthful alternative to other traditional candies. Serve pasteli as a light dessert or take them along as energy boosters on a hike.

Candy-Making
Notes:

The best-known Greek honey is made from wild thyme, and it is also the most common honey used for pasteli. But any honey will work; experiment with different varieties to find your favorites.

Recipe:

1 cup honey
1 teaspoon lemon peel
3 cups white sesame seeds, toasted

1. **Line a baking pan with parchment paper or a silicone baking mat.**

2. **Combine honey and lemon peel in a medium saucepan and bring to a boil over medium-high heat.**

3. **Add sesame seeds and stir to combine. Continue to cook until it reaches 250°F, hard ball stage.**

4. **Remove from heat and pour mixture into the pan. Use an offset spatula to spread the mixture as evenly as possible, about ½ inch thick.**

5. **When it has cooled and set, use a well-oiled knife to cut into pieces.**

Yield: About 20 pieces

Storage: Store in an airtight container between sheets of wax paper for up to 2 weeks.

---

49.   **PEPPERMINTS**

General Description: *Peppermints are refreshing candies made of nothing but peppermint extract and sugar.* Store-bought peppermints are easy to find, but homemade peppermints have a fresh, strong taste and are free of chemicals. Crushed peppermints are a common component of other desserts, mixed into peppermint ice cream, sprinkled over cakes and cookies, or substituted for the almonds in **almond buttercrunch**.

History: In ancient Europe and the Middle East, peppermint was often mixed with honey and used as a medicine, as was **horehound candy**. Peppermint candies were popular sweets in Europe in the mid-1800s. Brandy balls were a common variation, made with brandy, peppermint, and cinnamon. The Altoids brand of "curiously strong" mints were first made in 1837. But until the advent of chewing gum in the 1830s and Lifesavers Mints in the 1840s, peppermints were typically a homemade treat. Nearly every housewife had a recipe for easy peppermint candy.

Serving
Suggestions:

Serve fresh, homemade peppermint candies as an after-dinner sweet—alone or as an accent to a bowl of ice cream. Stock candy jars with instant breath fresheners. Peppermints can be crushed and used as an ingredient in **peppermint bark** or **peppermint marshmallows**.

Candy-Making
Notes:

Without food coloring, homemade peppermint is an amber-colored treat.

Recipe:

2¹/₄ cups sugar
1 teaspoon peppermint extract
Red food coloring, if desired

1. **Line a baking sheet with parchment paper or a silicone baking mat.**

2. **Combine sugar and ¹/₂ cup water in a saucepan and bring to a boil over medium-high heat. Continue to cook to 280°F, soft crack stage.**

3. **Remove from heat and stir in peppermint extract and food coloring.**

4. **Pour the mixture onto the baking sheet. Spread the mixture as evenly as possible, about ¹/₄ inch thick.**

5. **Let cool. Break peppermint into pieces.**

| Yield: | About 2 1/2 cups of peppermints |

| Storage: | Keep peppermints between layers of parchment paper in an airtight container for up to 2 weeks. |

---

50. **ROCK CANDY**

| General Description: | *Rock candy is simply made of large crystals of sugar clustered together on a stick, like a craggy lollipop.* This pure-sugar candy is tinted a rainbow of bright colors and commonly sold at North American candy stores and souvenir shops. |

| History: | Rock candy earned its name because sugar crystals resemble rock formations. It is often introduced to children as a science experiment that shows how crystals form. Since rock candy is pure sugar, it has many culinary applications: It is often used like granulated sugar in sweetening hot dessert soups in Asia, and it is mixed with aniseed and used as a breath freshener in India. Rock and Rye liqueur is sold with a large piece of rock candy in the bottom of the bottle, sweetening the liqueur. |

| Serving Suggestions: | By adding food coloring and flavorings to the sugar solution, you can make a rainbow of rock candies. This is a fun experiment to do with children as they can watch the crystals slowly growing over time. |

Candy-Making
Notes:

The sugar crystals will take several days to grow. The formation of uneven crystals is the process you prevent by beating candies like **fudge** and **fondant**.

Recipe:

4 cups sugar plus extra for coating sticks
Few drops food coloring, if desired
3 to 5 wooden sticks or bamboo skewers

1. **Find a large glass jar, taller than it is wide. Be sure it is completely clean and dry. Ensure the wooden sticks are long enough to stick out over the top of the jar.**

2. **Place 2 cups of water in a saucepan and bring to a boil at high heat.**

3. **Add the sugar 1 cup at a time, stirring until it is fully dissolved and the mixture is clear.**

4. **Add food coloring if desired.**

5. **Pour the sugar solution into the glass jar and let it cool for a few minutes. While you are waiting, wet the sticks in water and roll in sugar to coat. Let them dry. You are providing "seed" crystals that will encourage more sugar crystals to form.**

6. **Place the sticks in the jar, making sure the sugar solution covers several inches of them. Space them**

so there is room for sugar to grow. You can use clips or string to secure the sticks.

⧖ 7. **Cover the jar with foil. Store it at room temperature where it will be undisturbed for the next 5 to 7 days.**

8. **Remove candies when they are covered with big sugar crystals.**

Yield: 3 to 5 candies

▭ Storage: Store in airtight container for up to 2 weeks.

51. 📷 **SHERBET POWDER**

General Description:
A sherbet is a frozen dessert in some parts of the world, but sherbet powder is a British candy that produces a tingly, effervescent sensation in the mouth. When the powder is exposed to moisture, it dissolves and begins to fizz and bubble. Sherbet powder's fizzy sensation is similar to that of Pop Rocks candy, but Pop Rocks owe their "pop" to carbonation. Sherbet powder is quite easy to make at home and can add a little sparkle to your desserts.

History: Originally, *sharbat* was a medieval Arabic drink made from fruit juice, sugar, and ice, which made it very refreshing in hot weather. The drink travelled to western Europe and gained popularity there as well, becoming *sorbetto* in Italy, *sorbet* in France, and *sherbet* in England. In France and Italy, the drink evolved until the chilled fruit syrup became more solid than liquid, leading to the frozen fruit sorbets familiar to most people today. In Britain, the drink stayed in liquid form, but a clever seller of sherbet invented a fizzy powder that, when mixed with water, produced a bubbly, effervescent sensation.

Serving
Suggestions:
※ ☼

Add sherbet powder to any drink for a refreshing fizz similar to carbonation. Lemonade works particularly well, as does any fruit juice or fruit cocktail; chill drinks for the best effect. Eat sherbet powder straight like Pixy Stix, or eat it with a lollipop as a dipping stick like Fun Dip candy.

Candy-Making
Notes:

You can adjust the proportions of the citric acid to sugar to increase the sweetness or tartness of the mixture. Any added flavors must be dry so that they will not set off the chemical reaction. Flavor the powder by mixing it with any powdered drink mix. Then add water to turn it into a fizzy drink.

Recipe:

4 tablespoons confectioners' sugar, sifted
2 tablespoons citric acid (crystals or powdered)
1 tablespoon baking soda

1. **Combine all ingredients in a food processor and process until very fine.**

2. **Pour into a clean, dry container.**

3. **You can now taste the sherbet powder, add it to a drink, or roll drop candies in it to make sour candies.**

Yield: About ⅓ cup sherbet powder

Storage: Store in airtight container away from moisture.

---

52. **SPONGE TOFFEE**

General Description: *Its golden orange color and airy, spongy texture has earned sponge toffee a multitude of creative names.* This chocolate-covered confection is known as *honeycomb toffee* or *cinder toffee* in Britain, *sponge candy* or *sea foam* in America, and *hokey pokey* in New Zealand. It is made by cooking sugar and golden syrup or corn syrup to hard crack stage and then adding baking soda. The baking soda forms bubbles, giving the candy a foamy consistency that melts in the mouth.

History: Honeycomb toffee originated in Britain. Two popular commercial honeycomb toffee candy bars are the British Crunchie and the Australian Violet Crumble.

Serving
Suggestions:

This candy is typically served in large chunks covered in bittersweet chocolate. You can also cut them into elegant bars.

Candy-Making
Notes:

Golden syrup is a common sweetener in Britain and Australia; if you cannot find it, substitute molasses, honey, or corn syrup. When you add the baking soda, stir thoroughly to create as much aeration as possible.

Recipe:

1 cup sugar
3 tablespoons golden syrup
3 teaspoons baking soda
8 ounces bittersweet chocolate, optional

1. **Line an 8-by-8-inch baking pan with foil and butter well.**

2. **Heat sugar and syrup in a saucepan that's large enough for the mixture to bubble up after you add the baking soda. Bring the mixture to a boil over medium-high heat.**

3. **Continue cooking until the mixture reaches 285°F, hard crack stage.**

4. **Remove from heat and stir in the baking soda, mixing well to dissolve all of it. Be careful: the mixture will bubble up.**

5. **Pour the mixture into the prepared pan to cool. If you want, you can score the mixture with a knife as it cools.**

6. **Break the toffee into pieces. If desired, dip the toffee pieces in tempered chocolate (page 17), and place candies on a baking sheet lined with parchment or wax paper to set.**

Yield: About 24 pieces

Storage: Store in an airtight container for up to 1 week.

Creamy, Sticky, Chewy

53. ALMOND BURFI

General
Description:

This sweet, fudgey candy is eaten throughout India and Pakistan, especially at celebrations and other special occasions. Burfi, sometimes spelled *barfi*, is typically made by cooking milk until it thickens into a solid. Burfi is usually cut into small squares or diamonds covered with edible silver.

History:

Burfi means "snow" in Persian. This candy originated in Persia and was introduced to India during the Mughal dynasty in the 16th century. It is commonly served at Indian festivals, including Diwali, the Festival of Lights, and Holi, the Festival of Colors.

Serving
Suggestions:

Some of the most common flavors of burfi are coconut, pistachio, and saffron. You can make burfi with cashews instead of almonds or add shredded coconut to the batter. Another option is to use different food colorings in the batter to create a rainbow of choices for guests.

Candy-Making
Notes:

For authentic burfi, use *ghee*, or Indian clarified butter, instead of regular melted butter. Edible silver foil, called *varakh*, *varak*, or *vark* can be found at Indian groceries or online.

Recipe: 1 cup blanched almonds
          ¹/₂ cup milk
          ¹/₂ cup condensed milk
          6 tablespoons unsalted butter, melted
          ¹/₂ teaspoon almond extract
          Silver foil or slivered almonds for decorating

1. Line an 8-by-8-inch pan with foil and butter it well.

2. In a food processor or blender, grind blanched almonds to a fine powder. Add milk and mix into a fine paste.

3. In a saucepan, combine the paste, condensed milk, and almond extract over medium-low heat, stirring constantly for about 4 minutes.

4. Add the melted butter a few tablespoons at a time and stir to combine.

5. Stir in the almond extract. Cook for another 5 to 7 minutes, stirring until it is very thick and begins to come together in a ball.

6. Remove from heat. Put mixture into the baking pan and smooth out the surface. Garnish with slivered almonds or silver foil if desired.

7. **Let cool and set, about an hour, before cutting into pieces.**

Yield: About 25 pieces

Storage: Store in an airtight container for up to 1 week.

54. **BEIJINHOS DE COCO**

General
Description:
These charmingly named "little coconut kisses" are coconut candies given out at Brazilian parties as little signs of affection. Made from condensed milk and coconut, two classic ingredients in Brazilian cuisine, these bite-size confections are traditionally decorated with a single clove in the center. Their soft chewiness and rich coconut flavor make beijinhos a Brazilian favorite.

History: Portuguese colonists introduced sugar to Brazil, along with many recipes for candies and cakes. The giving of elaborately presented candies became a Brazilian tradition. Most of these candies have endearing names, such as *kisses* or *caresses*. *Beijinhos* is Portuguese for "little kisses"; *besitos de coco* are cookie kisses made from coconut and brown sugar.

Serving
Suggestions:
Coconut kisses can be coated in confectioners' sugar or more coconut. Nuts or chocolate kisses can be placed in the center instead of cloves.

1a. dark chocolate and nut bark
1b. peppermint bark

2a. chocolate bars
2b. filled chocolate bars

3. chocolate nougats

4a. vanilla bean chocolates

4b. jasmine tea chocolates

4c. ginger chocolates

5a. rich chocolate truffles
5b. white chocolate lemon truffles

5c. raspberry chocolate truffles
5d. mocha truffles

6a. caramel-filled chocolates
6b. mint ganache–filled chocolates

6c. Kirsch ganache–filled chocolates
6d. praline ganache–filled chocolates

7a. hollow chocolate rabbit

7b. Easter egg with treats

8a. mendiants
8b. white chocolate mendiants

9. mint meltaways

10. peppermint patties

11a. rochers
11b. coconut rochers

12. simple truffles

13. solid molded chocolates

14. agar jellies

15. apple jellies

16a. candied citrus peel
16b. orangettes

17. candied orange slices

18. candy apples

19a. caramel apple / 19b. dipped in chocolate and nuts / 19c. dipped in chocolate and sprinkles

20. chocolate-covered cherries

21a. chocolate-dipped strawberries

21b. tuxedo strawberries

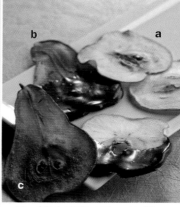

22a. dried apple and pear chips
22b. chocolate-dipped fruit chips
22c. fruit chips dusted with cinnamon

23a. fruit jellies

23b. Champagne jellies

24a. gumdrops

24b. gumdrop critters

25. gummy bears

26a. gummy worms
26b. sour gummy worms

27. licorice chews

28. marrons glacés

29. pâtes de fruits

30. stuffed dates

31. sugarplums

32. Turkish delight

33. acid drops (lemon drops)

34. butterscotch drops

35. candy cane twists

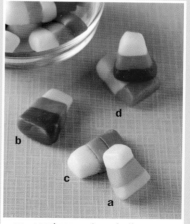

36a. candy corn / 36b. Indian corn
36c. reindeer corn / 36d. cupid corn

37. caramels

38. crystallized ginger

39. dulce de leche

40. English toffee

41. fleur de sel caramels dipped in dark chocolate

42. hard candy

43. honey taffy

44. horehound drops

45. humbugs

46a. lollipops

46b. round pops

47. maple candy

48. pasteli

49. peppermints

50. rock candy

51. sherbet powder

52. sponge toffee

53. almond burfi

54. beijinhos de coco

55. butter mints

56. buttermilk candy

57. chewy chocolate rolls

58. Chinese milk candy

59. cream cheese mints

60. daifuku mochi

61a. divinity
61b. sea foam divinity

62a. simple lemon-almond bonbons
62b. violet creams

62c. maple-walnut creams
62d. vanilla opera creams

63a. classic chocolate fudge
63b. opera fudge

63c. peanut-butter fudge
63d. penuche

64a. marshmallows
64b. candy-cane marshmallows

65. marshmallow chicks

66. Martha Washington candy

67. meringue mushrooms

68. molasses taffy

69a. nougat
69b. chocolate torrone

70. Oklahoma brown candy

71. pastillas de leche

72. saltwater taffy

73. almond buttercrunch

74. almond toffee bites

75. Chinese date-walnut candy

76. coconut-and-almond candy

77. croquant

78. dragées

79. French pralines

80. halva

81. Jordan almonds

82a. marzipan fruit

82b. marzipan pig

82c. marzipan hearts

83a. panforte di siena
83b. panforte nero

84. peanut brittle

85. peanut-butter brittle candy

86. peanut-butter cups

87. peanut patties

88. rum balls

89. Southern pecan pralines

90. turtle candy

91. candied flowers

92. candied nuts

93. caramel corn

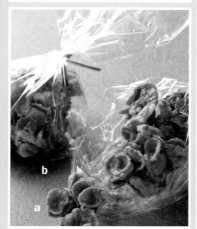

94a. cereal candy
94b. peanut-butter cereal candy

95. chocolate-covered coffee beans

96. chocolate-dipped potato chips

97. chocolate-dipped pretzels

98. chocolate fondue

99. chocolate peanut clusters

100. cinnamon candy

101. coconut haystacks

102. cow patties

103. crisped rice treats

104. date-nut roll

105. Easter egg nests

106. Irish potato candy

107. kettle corn

108a. **fondant cream mints**
108b. **double chocolate creams**

109. **no-fail fudge**

110. **nonpareils**

111a. **peanut-butter balls**

111b. buckeyes

112a. potato pinwheels

112b. needhams

113. rocky road

Candy-Making Notes:
The condensed milk and butter mixture has reached the proper thickness in step 2 when you are briefly able to see the bottom of the pan as you stir.

Recipe:
1 can (14 ounces) sweetened condensed milk
2 tablespoons unsalted butter
$^1/_2$ cup unsweetened coconut
$^1/_2$ cup sweetened flaked coconut
Sugar for rolling
Whole cloves for decorating, if desired

1. **Grease a baking pan or line with a silicone baking mat and set aside.**

2. **Combine condensed milk and butter in a saucepan and cook over medium-low heat, stirring until the mixture thickens, about 10 minutes.**

3. **Remove from heat and stir in the unsweetened and sweetened coconut.**

4. **Pour mixture onto baking pan to cool and firm up, about 30 minutes.**

5. **Using a small cookie scoop or your hands, roll into balls. Coat in sugar and place in candy cups. Place a single clove on top of each candy for decoration.**

Yield: About 50 coconut kisses

Storage: Store in an airtight container between sheets of wax paper for up to 1 week.

___

55. **BUTTER MINTS**

General
Description: *Dainty, petite butter mints are tinted with pastel colors and served as after-dinner sweets.* They are flavored with peppermint and are used like **peppermints** to freshen breath. However, butter mints are made with more butter, hence their name and soft, creamy taste. They are also known as *wedding mints*, *dinner mints*, and *pastel mints*.

History: Butter mints are commonly offered by restaurants to departing diners. A crystal bowl of butter mints, along with a bowl of **candied nuts**, can found at many weddings in the Southern United States.

Serving
Suggestions: A beautiful bowl of butter mints is always welcome at a party. They are also great favors for weddings; you can easily tint the mints to match the wedding colors.

Candy-Making
Notes: Butter mints are most often shaped in small rolls, but you can press the dough into molds or cut shapes with mini cookie cutters.

Recipe: ¹/₂ cup unsalted butter, room temperature
          1 tablespoon heavy cream
          3¹/₂ to 4¹/₂ cups confectioners' sugar
          ¹/₄ teaspoon peppermint extract or 1 drop
              peppermint oil
          Few drops food coloring, if desired

1. Line a baking sheet with parchment paper.

2. In a stand mixer with the paddle attachment,
    beat the butter and cream together until smooth.

3. Add the confectioners' sugar 1 cup at a time,
    and beat until it forms a smooth dough.

4. Add peppermint extract and food coloring and
    beat to combine. If you want several colors of
    mints, divide the dough into portions and add
    color to each portion separately.

5. Pinch off pieces of dough and roll them into long
    ropes about ¹/₂ inch thick. Use a knife to cut into
    small pieces. Place on the baking sheet and let set
    overnight before serving.

Yield: About 70 mints

Storage: Store in an airtight container in a cool, dry place for
          up to 1 week.

56. **BUTTERMILK CANDY**

General
Description:

Buttermilk candy is a soft, chewy, fudgy candy with the distinctive tang of buttermilk. This confection typically comes in irregularly shaped mounds and is studded with nuts. It is very similar to **fudge**; in cookbooks from the 1940s and 1950s the terms *buttermilk candy* and *buttermilk fudge* were often used interchangeably. When buttermilk candy is made with sour cream, it is appropriately called *sour cream candy*.

History:

Buttermilk candy is an old-fashioned American candy developed by experimentation and passed from generation to generation. The first recipes were published in the 1940s.

Serving
Suggestions:

You can vary the nuts used in the recipe; pecans will give it a praline-like flavor. Serve buttermilk candy alongside **fudge** during the holidays.

Candy-Making
Notes:

This recipe makes individual candy patties; turn this into a fudge by letting the mixture cool to 100°F after cooking and then beating vigorously until it loses its sheen.

Recipe:

1 cup buttermilk
2 cups sugar
2 teaspoons butter
1 tablespoon light corn syrup

⅟₄ teaspoon salt
1 teaspoon vanilla extract
1 cup walnuts, roughly chopped
1 teaspoon baking soda

1. Line a few baking sheets with parchment or wax paper and set aside.

2. Combine buttermilk, sugar, butter, corn syrup, and salt in a saucepan and bring to boil over medium heat.

3. Continue cooking until it reaches 248°F, soft ball stage.

4. Remove from heat and stir in vanilla extract and walnuts.

5. Stir in the baking soda. The mixture will foam up slightly.

6. Drop spoonfuls of the mixture onto the baking sheets. Let cool 30 minutes before serving.

Yield: About 30 candies

Storage: Store in an airtight container for up to 1 week.

57. **CHEWY CHOCOLATE ROLLS**

General
Description:
Chocolatey, fudgy, and chewy, Tootsie Rolls are iconic American candies that defy easy categorization. These Halloween perennials have a taste similar to chocolate and a firm, chewy consistency similar to caramels. The exact recipe for Tootsie Rolls is a secret, but chocolate-flavored candy rolls can be easily made at home.

History:
Tootsie Rolls were created in 1896 by Leo Hirshfield, who gave the candy his daughter's nickname, Tootsie. The Tootsie Roll became the centerpiece of Hirshfield's candy company, the Sweets Factory of America. In 1966 the name of the company was changed to Tootsie Roll Industries, Inc. Today, it is still one of the best-known and best-selling candies in America. Tootsie Rolls have an equally famous cousin, the Tootsie Pop, a spherical lollipop with a chewy Tootsie Roll center.

Serving
Suggestions:
These candies are a classic Halloween treat. Wrap them in decorative wax papers and mix them in the candy bowl with lollipops and caramels.

Candy-Making
Notes:
The original Tootsie Roll was flavored with orange extract for a citrus twist; add a few drops to this recipe if desired.

Recipe: 1 ounce unsweetened chocolate
1 tablespoon unsalted butter
$1/4$ cup light corn syrup
$1/2$ teaspoon vanilla extract
$1/2$ teaspoon orange extract
1 cup confectioner's sugar, sifted
$1/4$ cup instant nonfat dry milk

 1. **Melt chocolate and butter in a bowl over a pot of simmering water, stirring occasionally.**

2. **Stir in corn syrup, vanilla extract, and orange extract, and cook for 1 minute.**

3. **Remove bowl from heat. Stir in the confectioners' sugar and dry milk with a wooden spoon.**

4. **Turn out mixture onto a surface lightly sprinkled with confectioners' sugar. Knead the mixture until it becomes a stiff dough. Add up to $1/2$ cup more confectioners' sugar if it seems too soft to hold its shape.**

5. **Divide mixture into portions, and form each portion into a long, thin roll. Cut rolls into small pieces with scissors and wrap in wax papers.**

Yield: About 40 chewy chocolate rolls

Storage: Store in an airtight container in a cool, dry place for
up to 1 week.

58. **CHINESE MILK CANDY**

General   *Much of Asia has a fondness for mild, milk-flavored*
Description: *candies, and China's version is a beloved classic.* Called
White Rabbit Creamy Candy, this little white confec-
tion is a cross between taffy and Tootsie Rolls, with a
firm consistency that gradually softens to a pleasant
chewiness in the mouth. The sweet, lightly vanilla
flavor and lack of artificial ingredients or flavorings
make this a popular choice for parents to give their
children.

History: Milk-flavored candies are popular in many parts of
Asia, including China, Japan, and Korea. Part of their
appeal may come from the simplicity and pureness
associated with milk; candies that are "milk flavor"
are considered healthier than other sweets. White
Rabbit Creamy Candy was invented by Aipixi Candy
Factory in China in 1943. Its iconic rabbit icon and
name have made it one of China's most popular
sweets both at home and abroad.

Serving   These treats are often given out at Chinese New Year
Suggestions: or served in candy dishes for guests.

Candy-Making Notes:	Asian milk candies are traditionally wrapped in taste-less, edible rice paper that dissolves in the mouth.

Recipe: **2 cups sugar
1 cup light corn syrup
1 cup milk
2 tablespoons unsalted butter
$^1/_2$ teaspoon vanilla extract
Edible rice paper for wrapping, if desired**

1. **Coat a marble slab or baking sheet with cooking spray. Lightly spray a pair of kitchen shears. Have wax papers ready for wrapping the candy.**

2. **Combine sugar, corn syrup, milk, and butter in a saucepan.**

3. **Cook over medium heat, stirring constantly, until sugar is dissolved.**

4. **Continue cooking to 250°F, hard ball stage, without stirring.**

5. **Remove from heat. Turn out onto the prepared surface and let cool to room temperature. Turn the mass over a few times so it cools evenly.**

6. **Mix in vanilla extract.**

7. **Butter hands lightly and pull candy, stretching and gathering it until the mass becomes opaque and difficult to pull.**

8. **Pull the candy into a long rope about ¹/₂ inch thick, then cut it into bite-size pieces using the shears.**

9. **Wrap each piece in edible rice paper or wax paper.**

Yield: About 50 pieces

Storage: Store in an airtight container for up to 1 month.

59. **CREAM CHEESE MINTS**

General
Description: *Refreshingly minty and melt-in-your mouth soft, cream cheese mints are a popular after-dinner mint.* They are tinted in a rainbow of colors and formed into festive shapes for the holidays. Cream cheese has found fame as a spread for bagels and as the star component of cheesecake, but its soft consistency and mild tang make it a useful ingredient in baking and confectionery.

History: Philadelphia cream cheese is one of America's best-known contributions to the world of cheese. In Europe, American-style cream cheese is sometimes called *Philadelphia cheese.* Philadelphia cream cheese was developed in 1872 by dairyman William

Lawrence in an attempt to duplicate the French Neufchâtel cheese. The cheese Lawrence created was even softer and richer than Neufchatel.

Serving Suggestions:

Similar to **butter mints**, these candies can be served at wedding receptions or dinner parties. Tint the mints various colors to coordinate with the party's theme. Appropriately shaped candy molds, such as hearts, flowers, or baby bonnets add a lovely custom touch.

Candy-Making Notes:

When mixing the cream cheese and butter, keep them at the same temperature and softness so that they will blend together easily.

Recipe:

4 ounces cream cheese, room temperature
1 tablespoon unsalted butter, room temperature
4 cups confectioners' sugar, sifted
1/2 teaspoon peppermint extract or 1 drop peppermint oil
Few drops food coloring, if desired
Sugar for rolling

1. **Line a baking sheet with parchment or wax paper.**

2. **In a stand mixer with the paddle attachment, beat cream cheese and butter until just combined.**

3. **Add the confectioners' sugar, 1 cup at a time, and beat until it forms a smooth dough.**

4. **Add the peppermint extract and food coloring and beat to combine. For several colors of mints, divide the dough into portions and add color to each portion separately.**

 5. **Press the dough into candy molds. Let mints set for about 2 hours before unmolding.**

Yield: About 50 mints

Storage: Refrigerate in an airtight container between layers of wax paper for up to 2 weeks.

60. **DAIFUKU MOCHI**

General
Description: *Soft, sticky, sweet rice cakes,* mochi *are like the marsh-mallows of Japan.* Mochi come in many forms, from small round dumplings to delicately molded cakes, but they are always made from a glutinous rice flour paste that has a pleasantly chewy consistency. When mochi paste is sweetened and made into a confection, it is called *daifuku mochi*. The mochi paste is wrapped around a sweet filling, usually red bean paste or fruit.

History: Small cakes made of glutinous rice are found throughout Asia and Hawaii. The making of mochi has become a time-honored ceremony called *mochit-suki*; enthusiastic participants pound the rice into a paste with mallets. The Japanese confectionery tradition called *wagashi* includes daifuku mochi and other delicately formed sweets meant to be served with tea.

Serving
Suggestions:

The classic filling for daifuku mochi is red bean paste. One popular variation is *ichigo daifuku*, with a piece of fresh strawberry inside the mochi. Other fillings include jam, peanut butter, and Nutella. Serve daifuku mochi with tea for a Japanese snack.

Candy-Making
Notes:

When cooked, glutinous rice becomes sticky, unlike other types of rice. Glutinous rice flour can be used to avoid the traditional process of pounding rice. Glutinous rice flour and red bean paste can be found at Asian groceries.

Recipe:

2 cups glutinous rice flour
1/2 cup sugar
3/4 cup sweetened red bean paste, if desired
1 cup potato starch for dusting

1. **Combine rice flour, sugar, and 1 cup water in a microwave-safe bowl. Stir until just combined.**

2. **Cover the bowl with plastic wrap and microwave the mixture for about 3 minutes, until it has puffed up into a dough.**

3. **Let the mixture cool slightly and knead it a few**

times to form a smooth dough. Dust with potato
starch if it gets sticky.

 4.   **Pinch off a small piece of dough and press into a
rough circle about ¹/₄ inch thick. Place a spoonful
of red bean paste or other filling in the center and
form the dough around the filling, pinching the
edges shut.**

5.   **Roll mochi in potato starch to cover completely.
Repeat with the rest of the dough.**

Yield: About 12 mochi

Storage: Store in an airtight container for up to 1 week.

61a–b.   **DIVINITY**

General
Description: *With its white, cloudlike appearance and delicately
sweet taste, divinity leaves no doubt about the inspira-
tion for its name.* This fluffy confection is made from
a meringue of hot sugar syrup mixed with whipped
egg whites, which is beaten to incorporate as much air
as possible. Sometimes nuts are added; divinity with
pecans is a favorite in the American South. Divinity
is also referred to as *divinity fudge* or *divinity candy*.

History: Divinity became popular along with the development of corn syrup in the late 1880s in America. Most early divinity recipes use corn syrup as a partial substitute for the sugar usually used in making a meringue. Karo, one of the biggest makers of corn syrup, included recipes for divinity in recipe pamphlets attached to its bottles.

Serving
Suggestions:

Walnuts and pecans are common additions to divinity; many old cookbooks also have "Christmas divinity" recipes that include chopped nuts and candied fruit in the mixture. You can add about ¹/₂ cup mix-in ingredients in step 5. You can also spread the mixture into a baking pan and cut it into squares after it has firmed up.

Candy-Making
Notes:

It's best to make divinity on a dry, cool day. Humid weather prevents divinity from setting up properly— it will remain soft and sticky. If it becomes too hard and stiff, add a few drops of hot water and mix again to soften it.

Recipe:

2¹/₂ cups sugar
¹/₂ cup light corn syrup
¹/₄ teaspoon salt
2 egg whites, room temperature
1 teaspoon vanilla extract
1 cup walnuts, roughly chopped

1. Line several baking sheets with parchment paper or silicone baking mats.

2. Combine the sugar, corn syrup, $^1/_2$ cup water, and salt in a large saucepan. Cook over medium heat until it reaches a boil. Continue cooking until the mixture reaches 257°F, hard ball stage.

3. While the sugar is cooking, whisk the egg whites in a stand mixer with the whisk attachment at high speed, until stiff peaks form.

4. While the mixer is running, carefully pour the hot sugar syrup in a slow stream into the egg whites. Continue to whip until the mixture has cooled to room temperature and lost its glossiness.

5. Mix in vanilla extract and walnuts.

6. Using two moistened spoons, drop dollops of the mixture onto the prepared sheets.

7. Let set for about 1 hour until firm.

Yield: About 36 pieces

Storage: Store in an airtight container between layers of wax paper in a cool, dry place for up to 1 week.

Variation: ***Sea Foam Divinity***
Sea foam divinity is made by replacing the sugar in the recipe with brown sugar. The resulting candy has a light brown color which, combined with the bubbles from the whipped egg whites, gives it the appearance of sea foam.

62a–d. **FONDANT CANDIES**

General Description: *Most people think of fondant as a sweet covering for wedding cakes, but it's also a marvelously versatile candy.* It is made by working and kneading sugar syrup until it is a creamy, white dough; making fondant is similar to making **fudge**. In North America *bonbon* refers to fondant candy, whereas in Europe the word *bonbon* refers to all candies. Fondant candies are also called *French creams* in America.

History: Fondant was invented in the 19th century, much later than most confections. Dipped in chocolate, it became a popular candy in Europe and North America. Cookbooks from the 1950s to 1970s contain recipes for fondant flavored and rolled into balls, cut into patties, or formed into a loaf from which slices are cut. Today, fondant often decorates fancy cakes.

Serving
Suggestions:

The recipes on pages 179–82 suggest just some of fondant's many possible flavors and uses.

Candy-Making
Notes:

It is best to make this fondant on a dry day, since humidity can make it sticky. See also **no-cook fondant** as a simple alternative.

Recipe:

1 cup sugar
¹/₄ cup light corn syrup
¹/₄ teaspoon cream of tartar

1. **Combine sugar, corn syrup, cream of tartar, and ³/₄ cup water in a saucepan. Cook on medium heat until it reaches a boil.**

2. **Continue cooking to 238°F, soft ball stage.**

3. **Remove from heat and pour onto a marble slab or baking sheet. Let cool for several minutes until it is cool enough to touch.**

4. **Using a metal spatula or dough scraper, work the mixture back and forth until it turns solid white and has a soft, creamy texture, about 30 minutes.**

5. **Scrape the fondant into an airtight container. Refrigerate for at least 24 hours to let the fondant "ripen" and fully develop its pliable texture. Then**

it is ready to be used as desired.

Yield: About 1 cup

Storage: Refrigerate in an airtight container for up to 1 week.

Variations: ***Simple Lemon-Almond Bonbons***
These citrusy, slightly crunchy candies are one of
the simplest ways to use fondant. They pair well
with **truffles.**

1 cup fondant
¹/₂ teaspoon lemon extract or few drops lemon oil
1 cup sliced almonds, chopped fine

1. **Line a baking sheet with parchment or wax paper.**

2. **On a clean surface, knead the fondant until it is
soft and pliable. Knead in the lemon extract.**

3. **Shape it into 1-inch balls and roll in almonds to
coat. Place bonbons on the baking sheet to firm
up overnight.**

Yield: About 28 candies

Storage: Keep in an airtight container at room temperature for
up to 2 weeks.

Violet Creams

Floral-scented creams, especially these violet creams, are an English tradition. Use food coloring to tint the creams a shade of purple. Pair them with **candied flowers**, page 256.

1 cup fondant
¹/₂ teaspoon violet extract
Few drops violet food coloring

1. Line a baking sheet with parchment or wax paper.

2. On a clean surface, knead the fondant until it is soft and pliable. Knead in the violet extract and food coloring.

3. Shape the fondant into 1-inch balls and place on the baking sheet. Decorate with candied violets if desired. Let bonbons firm up overnight.

Yield: About 28 candies

Storage: Keep in an airtight container at room temperature for up to 2 weeks.

Maple-Walnut Creams

In the 1950s, maple was a popular flavoring for fondant. Roll the chopped walnuts into the fondant for a crunchy alternative.

1 cup fondant
2 teaspoons maple extract
1 cup walnuts, chopped fine

1. **Line a baking sheet with parchment or wax paper.**

2. **On a clean surface, knead the fondant until it is soft and pliable. Knead in the maple extract.**

3. **Shape the fondant into 1-inch balls and roll in the walnuts to coat. Place them on the baking sheet to firm up overnight before serving.**

Yield: About 28 candies

Storage: Keep in an airtight container at room temperature for up to 2 weeks.

Vanilla Opera Creams

Fondant centers dipped in tempered chocolate are called *opera creams* or *chocolate creams*. The names *opera creams* and *opera fudge* began appearing in cookbooks in the 1920s, although the origin of the names is unknown. Opera creams became particularly popular in Cincinnati, Ohio, and they are a specialty of the city to this day.

1 cup fondant
$^1/_2$ teaspoon vanilla extract

8 ounces bittersweet chocolate or coating
chocolate

🗒️ 🍫 1.   **Line a baking sheet with parchment or wax paper.**

2.   **On a clean surface, knead the fondant until it is
soft and pliable. Knead in the vanilla extract.**

🗒️ ⏳ 3.   **Shape the fondant into 1-inch balls and place on
the baking sheet. Let candy firm up overnight.**

🔥 🗒️ 4.   **Melt and temper the chocolate (page 17), or
simply melt the coating chocolate. Dip the fondant centers into the tempered chocolate. Place
back on the baking sheet to firm up.**

Yield: About 28 candies

🗄️ Storage: Keep in an airtight container for up to 2 weeks.

63a–d. 📷   **FUDGE**

General
Description: *This rich, sweet candy is one of the best-known and
beloved candies in America.* Fudge is a smooth,
creamy, semisoft candy made by cooking sugar and
dairy products together. The mixture is beaten as it
cools, which gives the finished candy its character-
istic smoothness. The most common flavoring for

fudge is chocolate; in fact, "fudge flavor" has become synonymous with chocolate flavor, but fudge can be flavored with many ingredients. Other common flavors include peanut butter, maple, butterscotch, and white chocolate.

History:

By most accounts the first fudge was created by accident in America, as a botched batch of caramels. Historians trace the name *fudge* to the late 1880s, when students at several New England women's colleges, including Wellesley, Vassar, and Smith, began making the candy in their dorms and selling it. The word *fudge*, which originally meant "to make dishonestly or carelessly," had by that time gained a new use as a mild exclamation ("Oh, fudge!"), and the students may have applied this word to their creation, paying tribute to the inadvertent origins of the candy.

Serving Suggestions:

The number and variety of fudge recipes found in cookbooks are astonishing. Several of the most popular variations are provided here.

Candy-Making Notes:

Good fudge depends on precise measurements and timing. A smooth, fudgy texture comes from the formation of small sugar crystals in the mixture after it cools to 110°F. If you do not cook the mixture to the right temperature or stir it too soon after cooking, too many large crystals will form too quickly, which leads to a grainy texture. The fear of bad fudge has led to the creation of many **no-fail fudge** recipes; these substitute ingredients such as evaporated milk or Marshmallow Fluff for the creamy texture of true fudge. However, the memorable quality of classic fudge makes mastering the recipe worthwhile.

Recipes: ***Classic Chocolate Fudge***

4 ounces unsweetened chocolate, chopped
3 cups sugar
¹/₂ cup milk
³/₄ cup cream
2 tablespoons light corn syrup
¹/₈ teaspoon salt
3 tablespoons butter
1¹/₂ teaspoons vanilla extract
1 cup nuts, chopped, if desired

1. **Line an 8-by-8-inch baking pan with aluminum foil and coat it with nonstick cooking spray.**

2. **Combine chocolate, sugar, milk, cream, corn syrup, and salt in a saucepan. Stir over medium-low heat with a wooden spoon until the chocolate melts and the mixture begins to boil.**

3. **Continue cooking without stirring until it reaches 236°F, soft ball stage.**

⏳ 4. **Remove from heat and add the butter. Do not stir. Let mixture cool to about 110°F.**

🥄 5. **Stir in the vanilla and nuts and beat vigorously with a wooden spoon or in a stand mixer until the mixture becomes thick and loses its shine.**

🍽⏳🔪 6. **Pour into the baking pan. Let set for 1 to 2 hours until firm. Cut into squares.**

Yield: About 16 squares

🍽 Storage: Store in an airtight container for up to 1 week.

Opera Fudge
This vanilla fudge is an excellent base for adding other flavors and ingredients of your choice.

2 cups sugar
1 cup heavy cream
2 tablespoons light corn syrup
1/8 teaspoon salt
3 tablespoons unsalted butter
2 teaspoons vanilla extract
1/4 cup candied cherries, chopped

🍽 1. **Line an 8-by-8-inch baking pan with aluminum foil and coat foil with cooking spray.**

2. **Combine sugar, cream, corn syrup, and salt in a saucepan. Stir over medium-low heat with a wooden spoon until the mixture begins to boil.**

 3. **Continue cooking without stirring until it reaches 236°F, soft ball stage.**

 4. **Remove from heat and add the butter. Do not stir.**

 5. **Add vanilla and candied cherries (if desired), and beat vigorously with a wooden spoon (or in a stand mixer) until the mixture becomes thick and loses its shine.**

 6. **Pour into the baking pan. Let set for 1 to 2 hours until firm. Cut into squares.**

Yield: About 16 squares

Storage: Store in an airtight container for up to 1 week.

Peanut Butter Fudge

2 cups sugar
1 cup milk
2 tablespoons light corn syrup
1/8 teaspoon salt
1/2 cup creamy peanut butter
1 teaspoons vanilla extract

1. Line an 8-by-8-inch baking pan with aluminum foil and coat foil with cooking spray.

2. Stir with a wooden spoon over medium-low heat until the mixture starts to boil.

3. Continue cooking without stirring until it reaches 236°F, soft ball stage.

4. Remove the pan and let mixture cool to about 110°F, about 30 minutes.

5. Add peanut butter and vanilla and beat vigorously with a wooden spoon (or in a stand mixer) until the mixture becomes thick and loses its shine.

6. Pour into the baking pan and let set 1 to 2 hours until firm. Cut into squares.

Yield: About 16 squares

Storage: Store in an airtight container for up to 1 week.

Penuche

This fudge is particularly popular in New England and the American South and is made with brown sugar for a caramel-like flavor. It is sometimes referred to as *brown sugar fudge*.

1½ cups light brown sugar
1 cup sugar
1 cup milk
1 tablespoon light corn syrup
2 tablespoons unsalted butter
¼ teaspoon salt
1 teaspoon vanilla extract
¾ cup toasted pecans, chopped

1. Line an 8-by-8-inch baking pan with aluminum foil and coat foil with cooking spray.

2. Combine the sugars, milk, corn syrup, butter, and salt in a saucepan over medium-high heat. Stir until the sugars are dissolved.

3. Continue to cook, stirring frequently, until the mixture reaches 238°F, soft ball stage.

4. Remove the pan and let cool to about 110°F, about 30 minutes.

5. Add vanilla and beat vigorously with a wooden spoon (or in a stand mixer) until the mixture becomes thick and loses its shine.

6. Stir in the pecans. Pour into the baking pan. Let set for 1 to 2 hours or until firm, and cut into squares.

Yield: About 16 squares

Storage: Store in an airtight container for up to 1 week.

64a–b. MARSHMALLOWS

General Description:

Whether toasted over a campfire, dropped into hot cocoa, or sandwiched into s'mores, marshmallows are one of childhood's best treats. These white, pillowy confections have a plush, spongy texture that comes from a hot sugar syrup being vigorously whipped with gelatin. Marshmallows are typically pure white and have a light vanilla flavor, but they can come in other colors and flavors, especially in France, where they are still handmade and sold in confectioneries.

History:

The word *marshmallow* first referred to a plant found throughout ancient Europe and Asia. *Pâte de guimauve* was invented by the French in the mid-1800s; *guimauve* is the French word for the plant. Made from the sap from the marshmallow plant whipped with sugar and egg whites, *pâte de guimauve* was the basis of the modern marshmallow. By the early 1900s, the marshmallow extract in marshmallows had been replaced with gelatin. Originally, marshmallows were manufactured in molds; an American candy company invented the extrusion process that produces the rounded marshmallows sold in stores today.

Serving
Suggestions:

No campfire is complete without marshmallows. Toast them and sandwich them between graham crackers and a piece of a **chocolate bar** for gooey s'mores. Top a mug of hot chocolate with marshmallows or use them to make **crisped rice treats**.

Candy-Making
Notes:

Try to time it so that the egg whites are whipped just as the sugar reaches the right temperature. If it seems the egg whites are whipping too fast, lower the speed or stop the mixer. Potato starch is best for keeping marshmallows from sticking, but a mixture of ¹/₂ cup cornstarch and ¹/₂ cup sifted confectioners' sugar also works well.

Recipe:

4 tablespoons unflavored gelatin
2 cups sugar
1 tablespoon light corn syrup
2 egg whites, room temperature
1 tablespoon vanilla extract
¹/₂ cup confectioners' sugar
1 cup potato starch

1. **Line a 9-by-13-inch pan with a piece of plastic wrap large enough to cover the bottom and sides and overhang the edges. Coat the wrap with cooking spray.**

2. **Combine gelatin with ³/₄ cup water in a bowl. Be sure the gelatin dissolves entirely and does not**

turn spongy. If necessary, microwave to keep it
liquid while you prepare the rest of the recipe.

3. Combine sugar, corn syrup, and 1 cup water in
a saucepan over medium heat until the sugar is
completely dissolved. Continue cooking without
stirring until the mixture comes to a boil.

4. Continue cooking until the mixture reaches 260°F,
hard ball stage. While the mixture is cooking,
place egg whites in the bowl of a stand mixer fitted
with the whisk attachment. When the sugar syrup
reaches 245°F, begin whipping the egg whites on
medium-high speed until they form firm peaks.

5. When the sugar syrup has reached 260°F, remove
from heat. Add the fully dissolved gelatin and
swirl to incorporate.

6. With the mixer on low, pour the sugar syrup in a
slow, steady stream into the egg whites; pour down
the side of the bowl to prevent splattering.

7. Turn the mixer to high speed and whip for 3 to 5
minutes until the mixture is very thick and glossy
white.

8. Stir in vanilla extract.

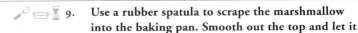

9.   Use a rubber spatula to scrape the marshmallow into the baking pan. Smooth out the top and let it set overnight at room temperature.

10. When you are ready to cut the marshmallows, combine confectioners' sugar and potato starch into a bowl. Sprinkle some of the mixture over a clean counter. Turn out the marshmallow onto the surface and dust the surface and sides liberally to prevent sticking.

11. Using a sharp chef's knife, cut the marshmallow into cubes. Run the knife under hot water and wipe clean between cuts to prevent sticking and keep the cut edges neat.

12. Roll the marshmallows in the mixture to coat.

Yield: About 16 marshmallows

Storage: Store in an airtight container for up to 5 days.

Variation: ***Candy-Cane Marshmallows***
Substitute 1 tablespoon peppermint extract for the vanilla. After pouring the marshmallow mixture into the pan in step 9, sprinkle a few drops of red food coloring across the surface. Use a toothpick to swirl the food coloring through the mixture.

65. **MARSHMALLOW CHICKS**

General
Description:

These soft, baby chick–shaped marshmallows are commonly found in Easter baskets across North America. Known as *Peeps*, they are made of a fluffy, creamy marshmallow that is piped into the form of a chick and then rolled in colored sugar. Bunnies, trees, and hearts can also be found. Today, Peeps are made by an automated process at the factory, but you can pipe your own handmade marshmallow chicks at home.

History:

Peeps were originally made by Rodda Candy in the 1920s. Just Born bought the company in 1953 and developed machines that automated the Peep-making process. The name *Peeps* may refer to the peeping sound made by chicks.

Serving
Suggestions:

These chicks are at home in Easter baskets. You can roll them in different colored sugars or pipe the marshmallow into different shapes.

Candy-Making
Notes:

This recipe does not use egg whites, resulting in a thicker, creamier marshmallow than the recipe on pages 190–92.

Recipe:

1 cup colored sparkling sugar for coating
4 tablespoons unflavored gelatin
2 cups sugar
1 tablespoon light corn syrup

1 tablespoon vanilla extract

1. Line a baking sheet with parchment paper and sprinkle with sparkling sugar.

2. Combine gelatin with ³/₄ cup water in a bowl. Be sure the gelatin dissolves entirely and does not turn spongy. If necessary, heat it in the microwave to keep it liquid while you prepare the rest of the recipe.

3. Combine sugar, corn syrup, and 1 cup water in a saucepan over medium heat until the sugar is completely dissolved. Continue cooking without stirring until the mixture comes to a boil.

4. Continue cooking until the mixture reaches 250°F, hard ball stage. Remove from heat. Add the dissolved gelatin mixture and swirl to incorporate.

5. Pour the mixture into the bowl of a stand mixer fitted with a whisk attachment. Whisk on high speed for 3 to 5 minutes until the mixture is very thick and glossy white.

6. Add vanilla extract and mix to incorporate.

7. Scrape the mixture into a large pastry bag fitted with a ¹/₂-inch round tip. Hold it at a 45° angle

over the baking sheet. Pipe a 3-inch line to form the body, releasing the pressure and pulling the bag up at the end to form a tapered tail.

8. Pipe the head by placing the pastry tip at the front of the body and pulling the tip back and then forward in an S shape. Release the pressure as you near the end to form the beak.

9. Sprinkle more colored sugar over the chick to coat before it dries.

10. Pipe the rest of the chicks and let them dry overnight at room temperature.

Yield: About 16 chicks

Storage: Store in an airtight container for up to 5 days.

66. MARTHA WASHINGTON CANDY

General Description: *These creamy, coconutty no-bake candies are pecan-studded balls of coconut and condensed milk that are dipped in chocolate, making them a cross between* **fondant candies** *and* **rum balls**. They often include chopped maraschino cherries.

History:	There is no proof that Martha Washington ever made this candy; perhaps the cherries inspired the name. Her surviving family cookbook contained recipes dating back to Elizabethan England. There are no recipes in the cookbook for chocolate candies, but there is a recipe for cherry preserves.
Serving Suggestions: ❀ ☼ ⟁ ❆	This easy-to-make candy is a good choice for a candy-making session with kids, as are **sugarplums**, **rocky road**, and **peanut butter balls**.
Candy-Making Notes:	Many older versions of this recipe call for dipping the candies in a mixture of melted chocolate and paraffin wax. This method was common in the early 1900s. The wax gave the chocolate a firm, glossy finish. Today, food-grade paraffin wax is available but generally meant for such purposes as sealing jars or coating fruit to make it shiny. There are better methods of making attractive dipping chocolate, including tempering chocolate and buying specially formulated coating chocolate.
Recipe:	**¹/₂ cup unsalted butter, room temperature** **7 ounces sweetened condensed milk** **16 ounces confectioners' sugar, sifted** **1 cup flaked sweetened coconut** **1 ¹/₂ cups pecans, roughly chopped** **¹/₂ cup maraschino cherries, chopped** **10 ounces semisweet or bittersweet chocolate**

1. In a stand mixer, beat butter and condensed milk on medium speed until smooth.

2. Add confectioners' sugar, 1 cup at a time, beating after each addition until fully incorporated.

3. Add coconut, pecans, and cherries and beat until just combined.

4. Cover and refrigerate for about 1 hour.

5. Line a baking sheet with parchment or wax paper.

6. Melt the chocolate in a metal bowl over a pot of simmering water, stirring occasionally. Remove from heat.

7. Form the mixture into 2-inch balls and dip into melted chocolate with a dipping fork. Place dipped candies on the baking sheet and let set until chocolate is firm, about 1 hour.

Yield: About 60 candies

Storage: Store in an airtight container between sheets of wax paper for up to 1 week.

67. MERINGUE MUSHROOMS

General Description:
Dainty meringue mushrooms are a sweet replica of the real thing. They are piped from a stiff batter and most often found adorning a yule log, a traditional Christmas cake.

History:
The yule log, or *bûche de Noël*, is a European Christmas tradition. A clever pastry chef noticed the resemblance of a jelly roll to a tree log and embellished the cake with frosting and decorations to enhance the resemblance. Over the years, chefs have made these traditional cakes ever more elaborate and fanciful, adding woodland creatures, holiday trimmings, and even Santa's sleigh. Meringue, a mixture of whipped egg whites and sugar, is prized as a soft, pipe-able decorating paste that dries to preserve the piped form.

Serving Suggestions:
Meringue mushrooms are at home on a yule log, a gingerbread house, or on the petits fours tray along with **marzipan** fruit.

Candy-Making Notes:
Do not worry about piping the mushrooms uniformly: Variation in size and shape only adds to the realism. To get rid of any unwanted peaks or ridges in piped meringue, smooth it with a moistened fingertip before it dries.

Recipe: 2 large egg whites, room temperature
$^1/_4$ teaspoon cream of tartar
$^1/_2$ cup sugar
1 ounce white chocolate
Cocoa powder for dusting

 1. Preheat oven to 250°F. Line two baking sheets with parchment paper and set aside.

2. In stand mixer with the whisk attachment, beat the egg whites until foamy. Add cream of tartar and whisk until soft peaks form.

3. With the mixer running, add the sugar in a slow, steady stream and whisk until the meringue holds very stiff peaks.

4. Place the meringue in a pastry bag fitted with a $^1/_2$-inch plain tip.

5. To pipe the caps, hold the pastry bag at a 90° angle to the baking sheet and pipe 2-inch rounds, releasing the pressure before pulling away for a smooth finish.

6. To pipe the stems, hold the pastry bag at a 90° angle to the baking sheet and pipe 1-inch cylinders, releasing the pressure as you pull up for tapered tops.

7. Bake the caps and stems for 45 minutes to 1 hour, rotating sheets halfway through. The mushrooms should be dry and firm to the touch. Let them cool completely on wire racks.

8. Using a toothpick, poke a small hole in the underside of each mushroom cap.

 9. Melt white chocolate in the microwave or in a metal bowl set over a pot of simmering water. Dip the top of each stem in the melted chocolate and insert into the hole of a mushroom cap. Place mushrooms cap down on a baking sheet to set, about 30 minutes.

10. Sift cocoa powder over the tops of the mushrooms.

Yield: About 30 meringue mushrooms

Storage: Store in an airtight container for up to 2 weeks.

68. **MOLASSES TAFFY**

General Description: *Richly flavored and amazingly chewy, molasses taffy is the original form of taffy.* It has a strong molasses flavor and dark brown color, unlike the variously colored and flavored **saltwater taffy**. Molasses taffy is firmer and even chewier than regular taffy because it is cooked longer.

History:

Molasses taffy, also called *pulled molasses candy*, was first made in the United Kingdom in the 1820s. By the 1840s, taffy-pulling parties were common social events. Young courting couples used the excuse of pulling candy to spend time in close proximity. The name *taffy* has evolved so that today British *toffee* and American *taffy* refer to very similar candies.

Serving Suggestions:

Since molasses taffy requires a lot of pulling, you could have an old-fashioned taffy-pulling party and send your guests homes with homemade taffy.

Candy-Making Notes:

This taffy recipe contains baking soda to produce bubbles that give the mixture a light texture. When you cut the taffy into pieces, wrap them in wax paper so that they do not lose their shape.

Recipe:

2 cups sugar
2 cups molasses
2 tablespoons unsalted butter
1 teaspoon salt
1/8 teaspoon baking soda
1/2 teaspoon vanilla extract

 1. Coat a marble slab or baking sheet with cooking spray. Lightly spray a pair of kitchen shears. Have

wax papers ready for wrapping the pieces of taffy.

2. **Combine sugar, molasses, 1 cup water, butter, and salt in a saucepan.**

3. **Cook over medium heat, stirring until sugar is dissolved.**

4. **Without stirring, cook to 260°F, hard ball stage.**

5. **Remove from heat. Stir in the baking soda and vanilla.**

6. **Turn out onto the baking sheet. Flip the mass a few times so it cools evenly to room temperature.**

7. **Butter hands and pull taffy, stretching and gathering it together until it becomes opaque and difficult to pull.**

8. **Pull the taffy into a long rope about ¹/₂ inch thick. Cut it into bite-size pieces using the shears.**

9. **Wrap each piece in wax paper. Let cool before storing.**

Yield: About 50 pieces of molasses taffy

Storage: Store in an airtight container for up to 1 month.

69a–b. ## NOUGAT

General
Description:

Nougat comes in an amazing variety of forms: hard, soft, chewy, studded with nuts, used as a filling, or eaten on its own. All nougats are made by whipping a hot sugar syrup with egg whites. This aerates and lightens the nougat. The mixture is then pressed into a compact slab and cut into pieces, which are wrapped in rice paper to prevent sticking. Nougat can be mixed with honey, nuts, or dried fruit. Classic nougat is white and tastes sugary sweet; dark versions are made with chocolate or caramelized sugar. The word *nougat* is also used as a general descriptor for the soft, whipped, chocolatey fillings in many commercial candy bars; see **chocolate nougats**.

History:

The first nougat was made in ancient Rome, Greece, or Persia. Nougat is most commonly found in southern Europe, especially Spain, where it is known as *turron*; in Italy, where it is called *torrone*; and in France, where it is *nougat*. Montelimar, France, is famous for its nougat. Nougat is also one of Provence's 13 Desserts of Christmas traditionally served on Christmas Eve.

Serving
Suggestions:

Bars of nougat are a festive addition to the Christmas table. Use a colorful mixture of nuts and dried fruits in the snowy white candy.

Candy-Making
Notes:

This recipe is for classic Italian white nougat torrone, which is firm and chewy, and made with honey and nuts. The firmness of the nougat depends on how hot you allow the sugar to reach in step 5: below 300°F for softer nougat, above 300°F for firmer nougat. Be sure to whip the mixture until it is quite stiff and holds it shape.

Recipe:

Edible rice paper, if desired
2 egg whites
$^1/_2$ cup honey
2 cups sugar
$^1/_3$ cup light corn syrup
$^1/_4$ teaspoon salt
1 teaspoon vanilla extract
2 tablespoons unsalted butter, room temperature
2 cups whole almonds, toasted

1. **Line a 9-by-13-inch baking pan with a sheet of rice paper or parchment paper.**

2. **In a stand mixer with the whisk attachment, beat the egg whites on high speed just until soft peaks form.**

3. **In a saucepan, cook honey over medium heat until it comes to a boil.**

4. **With the mixer on low, add honey. Continue**

whipping on high speed until the mixture has formed stiff peaks.

 5. Combine the sugar, corn syrup, ½ cup water, and salt in a saucepan. Cook over medium heat, stirring occasionally, until it reaches a boil. Continue cooking until the mixture reaches 300°F, hard crack stage.

 6. With the mixer on low speed, slowly pour the hot sugar syrup into the egg whites. Mix until stiff and glossy, about 5 minutes.

 7. Mix in vanilla extract and butter. The mixture may appear to separate; continue whipping, and it will reincorporate.

 8. Remove mixer bowl from stand. Using a wooden spoon or rubber spatula, beat in the almonds.

 9. Spread out mixture into the baking pan. Place a second sheet of parchment or rice paper on top, and then flatten the nougat with a rolling pin.

 10. Let nougat set overnight. Cut into pieces with a well-oiled knife.

Yield: About 36 pieces of nougat

Storage: Store in an airtight container in a cool, dry place for
            up to 1 week.

Variations: ***Chocolate Torrone***
            This is a rich, very chewy, chocolate version of the
            classic white nougat.

            Edible rice paper, if desired
            3 egg whites
            $1/2$ cup honey
            $1^1/2$ cups sugar
            $1/4$ teaspoon salt
            6 ounces semisweet chocolate, melted
            $1^1/2$ cups whole hazelnuts, toasted

1. **Line a 9-by-13-inch baking pan with a sheet of rice
    paper or parchment paper.**

2. **In a stand mixer with the whisk attachment, beat the
    egg whites on high speed just until soft peaks form.**

3. **Heat the honey in a saucepan over medium heat
    until it comes to a boil.**

4. **With the mixer on low, add the honey. Continue
    whipping on high speed until the mixture has
    formed stiff peaks.**

5. **Combine the sugar, $1/2$ cup water, and salt in a**

saucepan. Cook over medium heat, stirring occasionally, until it reaches a boil. Continue cooking until the mixture reaches 300°F, hard crack stage.

6. While the mixer is running, slowly pour the hot sugar syrup into the egg whites. Continue to whip until the mixture is stiff and glossy, about 5 minutes.

7. Add melted chocolate and whip to combine.

8. Remove mixer bowl from stand. Using a wooden spoon or rubber spatula, beat in the hazelnuts.

9. Spread out mixture into the baking pan. Place a second sheet of parchment or rice paper on top and flatten it with a rolling pin.

10. Let nougat set overnight before cutting it into pieces with a well-oiled knife.

70. **OKLAHOMA BROWN CANDY**

General Description: *Oklahoma Brown Candy is a cross between **fudge** and **caramels** that is a specialty of the Sooner State.* This crumbly confection looks like fudge and has a similar recipe, but Oklahoma brown candy incorporates caramelized sugar for a caramel flavor. The addition of pecans completes the rich sweetness of the candy. It is made by a unique method that encourages teamwork, making this a fun activity for parties.

History:

Legend has it that Oklahoma Territory pioneers were the first to make this candy that has become a treasured tradition for many Southern families. In Oklahoma, it is known as *Aunt Bill's brown candy*, though it is unclear who the namesake was. It is also known as *patience candy* because the lengthy process may try your patience; however, the result is well worth the effort.

Serving Suggestions:

There is a lot of stirring involved, so Oklahoma brown candy is an excellent group activity. Cut this rich, sweet candy into small pieces, and there will be plenty to go around.

Candy-Making Notes:

It's best to make this candy on a low-humidity day. Pour the melted sugar in a very thin stream and stir constantly to prevent it from clumping. If you have a helper, have one person pour the sugar and the other stir the mixture.

Recipe:

6 cups sugar
2 cups heavy cream
$1/4$ teaspoon baking soda
$1/2$ cup unsalted butter

1 teaspoon vanilla extract
3 cups pecans

1.   Line a 9-by-13-inch baking pan with foil and butter well.

2.   Place two cups of the sugar in a skillet. Combine the remaining 4 cups of sugar and cream in a saucepan.

3.   Cook the sugar in the skillet over medium-low heat until the sugar melts and turns golden brown. Stir occasionally to prevent the sugar from burning.

4.   Cook the sugar and cream mixture in the saucepan over medium heat until it reaches a simmer.

5.   Pour the melted sugar into the sugar and cream mixture in a very slow stream, stirring constantly. This can take up to 5 minutes; do not rush the process.

6.   Cook without stirring until the mixture reaches 246°F, firm ball stage.

7.   Remove from heat and stir in the baking soda. The mixture will bubble up.

8.   Add the butter and stir until it dissolves. Let cool for about 25 minutes without stirring.

9. **Add the vanilla extract and beat with a wooden spoon until the mixture becomes stiff and is no longer glossy, about 15 minutes.**

 10. **Add the pecans and stir to combine.**

 11. **Turn out mixture into baking pan. Let cool to room temperature before cutting into 1-inch squares.**

Yield: About 30 pieces

Storage: Store in an airtight container at room temperature for up to 1 week.

71. **PASTILLAS DE LECHE**

General Description: *This Filipino confection is as pure and creamy sweet as the milk it's made of.* Pastillas de leche are a simple candy made from boiling milk and sugar together into a soft paste, which is then formed into individual pieces and rolled in more sugar. These snowy white candies are traditionally wrapped in cellophane and white paper.

History: Pastillas de leche seem to be a version of **dulce de leche** since both terms mean "milk candy" in Filipino and Spanish, and both are made of milk and sugar.

But dulce de leche is cooked until it caramelizes and turns brown, and pastillas de leche are cooked slowly at a low temperature so they remain white.

Serving Suggestions:

The simplicity of this recipe makes it a wonderful candy to whip up anytime. Try using organic milk from a local creamery. The candy will taste of fresh, wholesome milk.

Candy-Making Notes:

These easy candies can be rolled into balls or cut into cylinders.

Recipe:

1¹/₂ cups milk
¹/₄ cup sugar
¹/₄ cup powdered milk
1 tablespoon lemon rind, optional
Extra sugar for rolling

1. **Combine milk and sugar in a saucepan over medium heat, stirring often, until the mixture becomes a thick paste.**

2. **Stir in powdered milk and lemon rind.**

3. **Remove from heat.**

4. **Roll into ¹/₂-inch balls. Roll balls in the extra sugar.**

Yield:

About 50 candies

| | | Storage: | These candies are traditionally wrapped in white wax paper. Store in an airtight container for up to 2 weeks. |

72. **SALTWATER TAFFY**

General
Description:

Renowned for its tooth-sticking chewiness and its association with the boardwalk in Atlantic City, New Jersey, taffy is a soft sugar candy available in a variety of fruit flavors. It is typically tinted with pastel colors, cut into bite-size pieces, and wrapped in wax paper. Taffy gets its incredible chewy consistency and stiff, sticky texture from the taffy-making process. **Molasses taffy** was its predecessor.

History:

Taffy originated in Britain and was brought to America in the 1800s. The term *saltwater taffy* was coined in a candy shop on the boardwalk in Atlantic City, New Jersey, in 1889. Saltwater taffy does not actually contain ocean water, and the taffy itself was not invented at the boardwalk, but the name has forever linked this candy with summer vacations by the sea.

Serving
Suggestions:

Taffy is a summertime treat. It can be flavored and colored to your preference: Try flavored oils such as peppermint instead of vanilla extract. Twist different colored ropes together to form multicolored taffy.

Candy-Making
Notes:
Pull the taffy mixture as much as possible; you may want to enlist helpers.

Recipe:
**2 cups sugar
2 tablespoons cornstarch
1 cup light corn syrup
2 tablespoons unsalted butter
1 teaspoon salt
¹/₂ teaspoon vanilla extract
Food coloring, if desired**

1. **Coat a marble slab or baking sheet with cooking spray. Lightly spray a pair of kitchen shears. Cut wax paper into 3-inch squares so that you'll be ready to wrap pieces of taffy in step 9.**

2. **Combine sugar and cornstarch in a saucepan. Add corn syrup, water, butter, and salt and stir to combine.**

3. **Cook over medium heat, stirring until sugar is dissolved.**

4. **Continue cooking to 260°F (hard ball stage), without stirring.**

5. **Remove from heat. Turn out onto the marble slab or baking sheet. Turn the mass over a few times to let it cool evenly to room temperature.**

6. **Divide taffy into portions if you want different colors and flavors. Mix in vanilla extract and coloring if desired.**

7. **Butter hands lightly and pull taffy, stretching and gathering it together until it becomes opaque and difficult to pull.**

8. **Pull the taffy into a long rope about $^1/_2$ inch thick. Cut it into bite-size pieces using the shears.**

9. **Wrap pieces in wax paper. Let cool before storing.**

Yield: About 50 pieces of taffy

Storage: Store in an airtight container for up to 1 month.

Nutty

73. **ALMOND BUTTERCRUNCH**

General
Description:

Thin slabs of toffee are covered with a layer of chocolate and sprinkled with almonds. The slabs are usually broken into irregular pieces. The decadent combination of hard, buttery toffee, rich chocolate, and crunchy nuts has made almond buttercrunch an American holiday classic.

History:

This delicious toffee confection is sometimes known as *English toffee*, but it is an American invention different from the true, original **English toffee**. One of the best-known commercial versions of buttercrunch is the Heath bar, which was created in 1928 by the Heath brothers in Illinois. A bar of hard toffee flecked with almonds and covered in milk chocolate, the Heath bar was originally marketed as a health food. Crushed bits of Heath bar have become a popular mix-in for cookies and ice cream. Other toffee candy bars include Skor, Butter Brickle, and Daim from Sweden.

Serving
Suggestions:

Almond buttercrunch is very similar to **chocolate bark** in that you can vary the type of chocolate and toppings: Try using pecans instead of almonds or adding crushed peppermint candies. Give tins of almond buttercrunch as holiday gifts.

Candy-Making
Notes:

Make buttercrunch on a dry day; humidity can make the toffee too soft and sticky.

Recipe:

³/₄ cup sugar
¹/₂ cup light brown sugar
¹/₂ cup unsalted butter, cut into pieces
¹/₈ teaspoon salt
¹/₄ teaspoon baking soda
1 teaspoon vanilla extract
12 ounces bittersweet or semisweet chocolate
2 cups slivered almonds, toasted and chopped

1. Line an 8-by-10-inch baking sheet with a silicone baking mat.

 2. Combine sugars, butter, vanilla, and salt in a saucepan. Cook over medium heat, stirring occasionally until it comes to a boil.

 3. Continue cooking without stirring until the mixture reaches 298°F, hard crack stage.

4. Remove from heat and stir in baking soda and vanilla.

5. Spread out the mixture on the baking sheet.

 6. Melt and temper the chocolate (page 17).

7. **Pour the tempered chocolate over the toffee layer. Sprinkle the almonds over the chocolate.**

8. **Let the toffee set for 1 hour before breaking into pieces.**

Yield: About 16 pieces

Storage: Store in an airtight container in a cool, dry place for up to 1 week.

74. ALMOND TOFFEE BITES

General Description: *Almond toffee bites are a cross between traditional English toffee drops and buttercrunch toffee.* Buttery toffee is mixed with almonds and formed into small logs, which are covered in chocolate and coated with more nuts. The most famous example of this candy is Almond Roca, made by Brown and Haley in Tacoma, Washington. Although the recipe is a company secret, it is easy to adapt a buttercrunch toffee recipe for homemade buttercrunch bites.

History: Brown and Haley dreamed up Almond Roca in 1923. They packaged it in distinctive pink metal tins to extended its shelf life, allowing it to be shipped around the world and earning the confection the nickname "the candy that travels."

Serving
Suggestions:
❀ ☀ ❆ ❄ ✄

Wrapped in decorative foils, these bites are a wonderful treat for guests. Use bittersweet instead of milk chocolate for a heightened contrast with the buttery-sweet toffee.

Candy-Making
Notes:
🔔

As with all toffees, this candy should be made on a dry day; humidity can prevent it from setting up, making it too soft and sticky.

Recipe:

1¹/₂ cups sugar
¹/₂ cup unsalted butter, cut into pieces
¹/₂ teaspoon salt
1 teaspoon vanilla extract
1 cup almonds, toasted and chopped fine
12 ounces milk chocolate
2 cups almonds, toasted and finely chopped

1. Line an 8-by-10-inch baking sheet with a silicone baking mat.

2. Melt butter in a saucepan over medium heat. Add sugar, 2 tablespoons water, vanilla, and salt. Stir occasionally until it comes to a boil.

3. Continue cooking without stirring until the mixture reaches 298°F, hard crack stage.

4. Remove from heat. Stir in vanilla and almonds.

5. **Spread the mixture on the baking sheet. After about 45 minutes, score into rectangles.**

6. **Break the toffee into individual pieces.**

7. **Melt and temper the milk chocolate (page 17). Place the remaining 2 cups of chopped almonds in another bowl. Line a baking sheet with parchment or wax paper.**

8. **Dip toffee pieces in milk chocolate and then roll in the chopped almonds. Place on the baking sheet to set before eating or wrapping in foil.**

Yield: About 16 pieces

Storage: Store in an airtight container in a cool, dry place for up to 2 weeks.

75. **CHINESE DATE-WALNUT CANDY**

General
Description: *These sticky, chewy little cubes are a time-honored Chinese confection.* A thick sugar syrup cooked with dates and walnuts sets into a dense, almost nougat-like slab packed with sweet, fruity flavor and nutty crunch.

History: Chinese confectionery is based on the use of fruits,

nuts, and seeds, rather than chocolate or sugar.
Peanuts, sesame, red bean, and ginger are common
ingredients in Chinese candy. Maltose, or malt sugar,
is the most common sweetener. It is only about one-
third as sweet as corn syrup, which is why Chinese
candies are generally much less sweet than their
Western counterparts.

Serving
Suggestions:

These not-too-sweet candies are wonderful as an
after-dinner nibble. They are a traditional treat at
Chinese New Year and are given as hostess gifts year-
round.

Candy-Making
Notes:

Maltose can be found at Asian groceries. Chinese
date-walnut candies are usually cut into individual
cubes or bars.

Recipe:

1 cup dried dates, pitted
1¹/₂ cup maltose
2 cups toasted walnut halves, roughly chopped
¹/₂ teaspoon salt

1. **Line an 8-by-8-inch baking pan with plastic wrap**
   and coat it with cooking spray. Set aside.

2. **Combine dates and 2 cups of water in a saucepan**
   and bring to a boil over high heat. Reduce heat
   and cook for 10 minutes until the dates are a
   jammy consistency.

3. **Drain excess liquid from the date mixture, leaving the dates in the saucepan. Add maltose, walnuts, and salt, and, stirring occasionally, cook over medium heat for 10 minutes or until the mixture is very thick.**

 4. **Pour the mixture into the baking pan and let it set overnight at room temperature.**

 5. **Flip the pan onto a clean work surface. Peel off the plastic wrap, and cut the candy into 1-inch pieces.**

Yield: About 40 pieces

 Storage: Store in an airtight container in a cool, dry place for up to 1 week.

---

76. **COCONUT-AND-ALMOND CANDY**

General Description: *The killer combination of coconut, almonds, and milk chocolate makes for a delectable candy bar.* One of the most iconic American candies, the Almond Joy, is famous for its creamy coconut filling topped with almonds and covered in milk chocolate. Its sibling, the Mounds bar, has the same coconut center but no almonds. Although the recipes for these two candies are top secret, it's possible to make wonderfully coconutty chocolate candies in your own home.

History:

The Almond Joy was invented in 1946 by the Peter Paul Candy Manufacturing Company in Connecticut. The Mounds bar was the original version of the candy, premiering in 1921. Peter Paul used the unusual strategy of creating two very similar candies and advertising them as competing versions, encouraging consumers to pick a favorite. This tactic worked: Almond Joy and Mounds became two of the best-selling candies in the 1920s.

Serving Suggestions:

Trick-or-treaters will be delighted to find these candies in the Halloween candy bag. Wrap them in foil or place them in candy cups.

Candy-Making Notes:

You can eliminate the almonds and cover the coconut centers with dark chocolate. Better yet, make both versions and give your guests a pleasant dilemma of which to choose.

Recipe:

7 fluid ounces sweetened condensed milk
1 teaspoon vanilla extract
1/8 teaspoon salt
2 1/4 cups confectioners' sugar
14 ounces sweetened flaked coconut
1/2 cup whole almonds, toasted
16 ounces milk chocolate or coating chocolate

1. Line a 9-by-13-inch pan with foil and coat it with nonstick cooking spray.

2. Combine condensed milk, vanilla extract, and salt in a bowl.

3. Add confectioners' sugar 1 cup at a time and stir with a wooden spoon until fully incorporated.

4. Add coconut and stir until combined.

5. Pour the mixture into the baking pan and press it into an even layer. Then press the almonds into the mixture in even rows. Chill candy in refrigerator until firm, about 1 hour.

6. Using a sharp chef's knife, cut the candy into small rectangles.

7. Line a baking sheet with parchment or wax paper.

8. Melt and temper the chocolate (page 17), or simply melt the coating chocolate.

9. Dip the bars into the chocolate, covering completely, and place them on the prepared sheet.

10. Refrigerate candy for 30 minutes or until the chocolate has set.

Yield:	About 40 candies
Storage:	Store in an airtight container in a cool, dry place for up to 1 week.

77. CROQUANT

General
Description:

Croquant—the French version of brittle—is made of delicate, wafer-thin sheets of caramelized sugar studded with slivers of nuts. Whereas the North American brittles are meant to eaten on their own, croquant is typically used as a garnish or ingredient for other desserts. Like **praline**, it is ground into shards or a fine powder and used as a layer in cakes or a filling for chocolates. Some chefs use the terms *croquant* and *nougatine* interchangeably; both refer to a confection that can be enjoyed as a petit four or used to add a crisp, nutty filling to a dessert.

History:

Croquant means "crunchy" in French, which makes the name as appropriate for this confection as the English "brittle." However, sometimes *croquant* is used in France to refer to similarly crunchy candies or foodstuffs. *Nougatine* is a darker, denser version of nougat made only with sugar and nuts, but it is nearly identical to croquant.

Serving
Suggestions:

Substitute other nuts for the almonds if you wish;
just be sure they are finely chopped so the croquant
will be thin. Pieces of croquant are the perfect way
to top a cake or scoop of ice cream. You can also
spread a layer of tempered chocolate on one side, like
almond buttercrunch, for a rich, indulgent treat.

Candy-Making
Notes:

Like all brittles, croquant is sensitive to humidity
and best made on a dry day. If the weather is humid,
the brittle may not set up properly and will remain
sticky and chewy.

Recipe:

1 cup sugar
2 tablespoons unsalted butter
$1/2$ teaspoon vanilla extract
$1/8$ teaspoon salt
1 cup sliced almonds

1. **Line a baking sheet with a silicone baking mat or
coat with cooking spray.**

2. **Place sugar and $1/4$ cup water in a saucepan, with
the sugar completely covered with water. Bring it
to a boil over high heat.**

3. **Continue cooking until mixture reaches 250°F.
Add butter, vanilla extract, and salt and stir
to combine.**

4. **Continue cooking until mixture reaches 290°F.
Remove from heat and stir in almonds.**

 5. **Pour mixture onto the baking sheet, spreading as
evenly and thinly as possible.**

6. **When croquant has set, break into pieces.**

Yield: About 50 pieces

Storage: Store in an airtight container at room temperature for
up to 1 week.

78. 📷 **DRAGÉES**

General
Description:
*Dragées are nuts or other sweet treats that have been
coated with a sugary shell.* The word *dragée* comes
from the French for "to dredge"—an appropriate
name since the candy is made by dredging nuts
through a sweet coating. **Jordan almonds** are the
best-known dragées, and the two terms have become
nearly synonymous. Any sugar-coated confection can
be called a dragée; the French consider **pralines** to be
dragées. One version takes the praline a step further
and covers the nuts in chocolate and cocoa powder,
creating a rich, indulgent treat. This form of dragée
is the easiest to reproduce at home, and is the recipe
given on the opposite page.

History:	Sugar-coated nuts have been eaten at celebrations since the Middle Ages. Today, dragées are also known as *panned candies* because most commercial dragées are made by placing the nuts in a large pan or other container and agitating it while the coating is poured in so that the nuts are evenly coated. The resulting candy has a perfectly round, smooth coating. Other panned candies include M&Ms, jellybeans, and the tiny metallic-colored sugar balls used to decorate cookies and cakes.
Serving Suggestions:	Serve dragées with cocktails or as an after-dinner sweet. For extra kick, add ¹/₂ teaspoon of cinnamon or cayenne pepper to the nuts when you toss them in caramel (step 4).
Candy-Making Notes:	Watch the cooking sugar to prevent scorching. Since it is not mixed with water, it will cook quickly.
Recipe:	**2 cup sugar** **4 cups whole almonds** **12 ounces semisweet chocolate** **¹/₂ cocoa powder, sifted**

1. **Line several baking sheets with foil or silicone baking mats.**

2. **Place sugar in a saucepan and cook over medium-low heat, stirring occasionally until it is melted.**

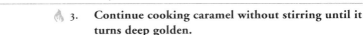

3. Continue cooking caramel without stirring until it turns deep golden.

4. Add almonds, stirring until coated well.

5. Use a spatula to spread the nuts on baking sheets, separating them from one another. Let cool.

6. When the almonds are cool, place them in a bowl. Melt and temper the chocolate (page 17).

7. Pour tempered chocolate over the nuts and stir to coat.

8. When the chocolate has almost set on the nuts, add cocoa powder and stir to coat. It may be easiest to toss the nuts with your hands.

9. Toss the nuts in a sieve or sifter if necessary to eliminate any clumps. Place nuts in a single layer on baking sheets to dry.

Yield: 4 cups of nuts

Storage: Store in an airtight container for up to 2 weeks.

79. 📷 **FRENCH PRALINES**

General Description:	*French pralines are the original finger food: whole almonds lightly coated with caramelized sugar.* Although almonds are the nuts traditionally used for pralines, hazelnuts are common as well. In Europe pralines are often ground into a powder called *pralin* or into a thicker praline paste, both of which are used to flavor desserts and chocolates. European chocolates filled with *pralin* or praline paste are often called *pralinés*; the ubiquity of the name is a tribute to the popularity of this flavor. **Southern pecan pralines** are made with pecans and brown sugar.
History:	Sugar-coated nuts have been enjoyed across Europe and the Middle East since the Middle Ages, but pralines were invented in France in the 17th century at the estate of the Duke of Plesiss-Praslin, a sugar industrialist. Legend has it that his cook came up with idea of coating almonds with caramelized sugar; the duke took the candy to the court of Louis XIII and promptly had it named after him. The cook later retired from the duke's service and opened his own shop in Montargis, Maison de la Praline ("House of Praline"), which is still open today.
Serving Suggestions:	Pralines are perfect hors d'oeuvres or after-dinner sweets. Crushed pralines can top ice cream, cakes, and cupcakes.

Candy-Making ⚠ Notes:	Watch the cooking sugar to prevent scorching. Since it is not mixed with water, it will cook quickly.	

Recipe: **2 cup sugar**
3 cups whole almonds

🍱 I. **Line several baking sheets with foil or silicone baking mats.**

🥘🔥🥄 2. **Place sugar in a saucepan and cook over medium-low heat, stirring occasionally until it melts and starts turning golden.**

🥄 3. **Add almonds, stirring to coat.**

🍱🥄 4. **Turn out almonds onto baking sheets. Use a spatula to spread the nuts, separating them from each other. Let cool.**

Yield: About 3 cups of pralines

🗄 Storage: Store in an airtight container in dry, cool place for up to 3 weeks.

---

80. 📷 **HALVA**

General
Description: Halva *is the general term for a very wide range of sweets consumed across the Balkans, Middle East, central Asia,*

and India. It is also a popular Jewish treat, often spelled *halvah* or *chalvah*. The two most common forms of halva are a thick pudding-like dessert made with ground semolina, honey, butter, and dried fruit, most popular in Greece and India, and a chewier, fudgelike confection made from sesame seeds, honey, and tahini, most common in the Balkans and Middle East. Flavorings and other ingredients are added depending on the region, making halva a truly international candy.

History: *Halva* comes from the Arabic word *halwa*, meaning "sweet." The earliest forms of halva were made in Turkey of ground semolina flour cooked with honey or sugar. The candy was eagerly adopted by India as well as by Jewish populations in the Balkans. As it travelled from region to region, halva was adapted to local tastes, ingredients, and cooking techniques.

Serving Suggestions: Halva is served at numerous special occasions and festivals around the world, from Jewish Purim to Hindu Diwali. It can be enjoyed year-round as a simple, healthy snack.

Candy-Making Notes: This recipe is for a sesame halva, the type made in Israel. Jewish immigrants brought it to America.

Recipe: **¹/₂ cup sesame oil**
2 cups all-purpose flour

1 cup tahini paste
$^1/_2$ cup honey
$^1/_4$ cup sesame seeds

1. Coat a 5-by-9-inch loaf pan with cooking spray and set aside.

2. Combine sesame oil and flour in a skillet and cook over low heat until the mixture turns light brown.

3. Add the tahini paste and stir to combine. Remove from heat and set aside.

4. Place honey in a small saucepan and cook on medium heat until it reaches 238°F, soft ball stage.

5. Pour honey into the flour mixture and stir to combine. Add the sesame seeds and stir to combine.

6. Spread out mixture in the baking pan. Let cool until firm, about 2 hours.

7. Using an oiled chef's knife, slice into pieces.

Yield: About 15 pieces

Storage: Store between sheets of wax paper in an airtight container in a dry, cool place for up to 2 weeks.

81. 📷 **JORDAN ALMONDS**

General Description:	*Jordan almonds have crisp, pastel-colored sugar shells and are a common sight at weddings and other elegant functions.* They are also known as *sugared almonds* or *almond dragées*, and as *confetti* in Italy and *koufeta* in Greece. These candies did not originate in Jordan: The name refers to the Jordan variety of almond.
History:	Ancient Romans gave out honey-covered nuts at festivities. When sugar became commonly available in Europe in the 15th century, it became common practice to coat nuts in sugar. Sugared nuts became popular at weddings from the Middle East through southern Europe, especially Italy. In the town of Sulmona, the Pelino family refined the technique of coating the almonds in sugar to create the familiar sugar-shelled candies. Today, the Confetti Pelino Company still makes them for Italian brides.
Serving Suggestions:	Jordan almonds are a common favor at wedding celebrations worldwide. It is traditional in Italy and most other parts of Europe to give out small bags containing five almonds, representing happiness, health, longevity, wealth, and fertility.
Candy-Making Notes:	Whereas modern Jordan almonds have a candy coating, the traditional *confetti* made in Italy use nothing

more than sugar to create the shell. This recipe uses a simple fondant coating.

Recipe: **2¹/₂ pounds whole blanched almonds**
1 pound confectioners' sugar
3 egg whites
Food coloring if desired

1. **Preheat the oven to 350°F. Spread out almonds on several baking sheets. Toast them for 5 to 10 minutes, until you can smell them toasting. Remove from oven and let cool.**

2. **Line clean, cool baking sheets with silicone baking mats.**

3. **In a stand mixer with the paddle attachment, beat sugar and egg whites together until thick. Add food coloring if desired.**

4. **Coat almonds with the fondant mixture.**

5. **Place nuts on baking sheets to dry.**

Yield: About 4 cups of candy

Storage: Refrigerate in an airtight container for up to 3 weeks.

82a–c. **MARZIPAN**

General
Description:

Marzipan is a soft, sweet, almond-flavored paste that can be shaped into virtually any form. Rich and nutty, it is made from ground almonds, egg whites, and confectioners' sugar. It is used to fill chocolates and cover cakes, much like **fondant**. This versatile candy can also be flavored, colored, and layered like bar candy.

History:

Marzipan was invented in the Middle East and introduced to Europe in the Middle Ages. European confectioners used it to sculpt edible centerpieces and treats. In Britain, beautiful models made from *marchpane* (the British term for the candy) were fashionable at parties in the 15th century. In the Middle East, the confection is known as *lozina*; the word *marzipan* may have evolved from the Italian term *marzapane*. Centuries after its invention, marzipan is still a popular candy worldwide.

Serving
Suggestions:

Use molds to form the candy or shape it with your hands. Marzipan hearts make a lovely Valentine's Day gift. In Germany, marzipan pigs are given at Christmas and New Year's. In Italy, it is colored and shaped into replicas of fruit. In the Middle East, marzipan is flavored with rosewater and orange flower and formed into delicate blossoms.

Candy-Making Notes:	There are several types of marzipan: The most basic form is a combination of ground almonds and sugar; the French form combines ground almonds with a hot sugar syrup for a softer, lighter paste; and this recipe uses ground almonds, confectioners' sugar, and egg whites to create a firm but pliable dough.
Recipe:	**1¹/₂ cups blanched almonds** **4 cups confectioners' sugar, divided** **2 egg whites** **¹/₂ teaspoon almond extract, rosewater, or other flavoring**

1. **Combine the almonds and about 1 cup confectioners' sugar in a food processor. Process until the almonds are very fine, about 2 minutes.**

2. **Add the egg whites, and process until the mixture turns into a smooth paste.**

3. **Add the remaining confectioners' sugar a cup at a time, processing it in to form a smooth ball of dough. Add more confectioners' sugar if it is sticky, less if it is already firm and pliable.**

4. **Add the almond extract, and process to combine.**

5. **Use the marzipan or save it for later use.**

Yield: About 1 pound of marzipan

Storage: Store wrapped in plastic in an airtight container in the refrigerator for up to 1 month.

Variations: **Marzipan Fruit**
Divide the marzipan into several portions, one for each color. Tint each portion with a few drops of food coloring and knead it until you have the desired shade.

Apple: Make a ball of red marzipan and use a small wooden dowel or skewer to make an indentation at the top and bottom. Insert cloves in the indentations.

Strawberry: Make a ball of red marzipan and form into a strawberry shape, with one wide one and one pointy end. Roll in sparkling red sugar. Add a stem of green marzipan.

Citrus fruit: Make a ball of yellow, orange, or green marzipan and form into the appropriate shape. Roll the fruit lightly over a grater to create a nubbly, dimpled texture. Add a clove at the top of the fruit.

Marzipan Pig
In parts of Europe, marzipan pigs are given as sweet treats during Christmas. Use a flexible candy mold in the shape of a pig. Tint the marzipan pink with a few drops of red food coloring.

Marzipan Hearts

Line several baking sheets with parchment paper or silicone baking mats. Cover a work surface in confectioners' sugar, and roll out the marzipan to ¼ inch thick. Use a cookie cutter to cut out heart shapes. Place on prepared sheets. Decorate with icing, miniature candies, or sprinkles.

83a–b. **PANFORTE DI SIENA**

General
Description:

Panforte is a cross between cake and candy and a classic Christmas treat from the Tuscan town of Siena. Made from nuts, candied fruit, and spices combined with sugar and honey syrup, this confection is rich, spicy, and very chewy. Although traditional panforte does not contain chocolate, many popular modern versions do. It is usually shaped in a round and served in slices like cake, but its dense texture and intense sweetness make it similar to chewy candies. Panforte also invites comparisons to English fruitcake, with its candied fruit and long shelf life.

History:

The word *panforte* means "strong bread" in Italian; "strong" refers to the powerful spiciness of the confection. The original form of panforte was *panpepato*, or "pepper bread"; it contained generous amounts of spices, including pepper, which were valued commodities imported from the Middle East. Panforte was first created in Siena during the 13th century, and it has been enjoyed as a special Italian Christmas treat since.

Serving
Suggestions:

Panforte is traditionally dusted with confectioner's sugar and served in small wedges. It is best enjoyed with a glass of vin santo or port.

Candy-Making
Notes:

Experiment with a combination of nuts, dried fruit, and spices that you like—just be sure to keep the total amount of mix-ins the same.

Recipe:

1 cup almonds, toasted and coarsely chopped
1 cup hazelnuts, toasted, skinned, and coarsely chopped
1 cup candied orange peel, citron, or lemon peel, coarsely chopped
$^1/_2$ cup all-purpose flour
$^1/_2$ teaspoon cinnamon
$^1/_4$ teaspoon cloves
$^1/_4$ teaspoon coriander
$^1/_4$ teaspoon nutmeg
$1^1/_4$ cup sugar
$^1/_2$ cup honey
Confectioners' sugar for dusting

1. **Preheat the oven to 300°F. Grease an 8-inch round springform pan or line an 8-inch round cake pan with foil and grease well.**

2. **Combine nuts, candied peel, flour, and spices in a bowl.**

 3. **Combine sugar and honey in a saucepan and bring to a boil over medium heat.**

 4. **Continue cooking the sugar syrup until it reaches 242°F, firm ball stage. Immediately pour it over the nut mixture and stir until fully combined.**

5. **Turn out the mixture into the cake pan and spread evenly.**

6. **Bake for 30 to 35 minutes until the mixture is bubbling around the edges.**

7. **Let pan cool before removing the springform ring or pulling the panforte from the cake pan. Dust the top liberally with confectioners' sugar before serving.**

Yield: One 8-inch round of panforte

Storage: Wrap in aluminum foil and store in an airtight container for up to 1 month.

Variation: **_Panforte Nero_**
For chocolate panforte, add 2 tablespoons of cocoa powder in step 2.

84. **PEANUT BRITTLE**

General
Description:

All brittles have a crisp crunchiness that make them delightfully addictive. They are made from sugar syrup cooked to hard crack stage like **hard candy** and then mixed with nuts. The mixture is then poured very thinly so it will break easily into crunchy shards. Sometimes baking soda is added to aerate it so it is easier to bite into. Although in America peanut brittle is the most popular version, almost any nut can be used, making brittle one of the easiest ways to combine sugar and nuts into one delicious candy.

History:

Many brittle-like candies are made with nuts covered in honey or sugar syrup, such as Greek **pasteli** or French **croquant**. Brittles are made with pistachios and almonds in the Middle East and sesame seeds and peanuts in Asia.

Serving
Suggestions:

Brittle can be enjoyed on its own, but it also makes a wonderful garnish for desserts. Use different nuts—such as cashews or almonds—to complement your ice creams or cakes.

Candy-Making
Notes:

This recipe has you pull the brittle mixture like a taffy, giving it a lovely airy texture. Use extreme caution when handling the hot brittle mixture, and wear rubber gloves to protect your hands. Brittle is best made on a dry day; humidity can prevent it from setting up.

Recipe: **2 cups sugar**
1 cup light corn syrup
1 teaspoon vanilla extract
¹/₈ teaspoon salt
2 cups raw Spanish peanuts
2 teaspoons baking soda

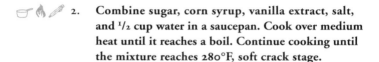

1. **Grease a large baking sheet and set aside.**

2. **Combine sugar, corn syrup, vanilla extract, salt, and ¹/₂ cup water in a saucepan. Cook over medium heat until it reaches a boil. Continue cooking until the mixture reaches 280°F, soft crack stage.**

3. **Stir in peanuts. Reduce to medium-high heat and cook for 12 to 15 minutes, stirring frequently, until the mixture reaches 300°F, hard crack stage.**

4. **Remove from heat and stir in the baking soda.**

5. **Spread mixture on the baking sheet with a spatula.**

6. **When the candy has cooled enough to handle but is still hot, butter your hands and pull the brittle from all sides until it is very thin.**

7. **When the brittle is cool, break into pieces.**

Yield: About 2 pounds of brittle

Storage: Store in an airtight container for up to 2 weeks.

85. **PEANUT-BUTTER BRITTLE CANDY**

General
Description: *Adding peanut butter to brittle gives it a soft, creamy texture, and covering peanut butter brittle in chocolate makes it an irresistible candy bar.* The Butterfinger bar is a popular American candy with a crisp peanut butter center covered in chocolate. Although the exact Butterfinger recipe is unknown, it is possible to make a similar candy by mixing peanut butter with a classic brittle-making technique. This is a crunchy, flaky candy with intense peanut butter flavor.

History: Butterfinger was created by the Curtiss Candy Company in 1923. This Chicago candy company also invented the Baby Ruth candy bar. When Curtiss Candy Company was sold to Nabisco in 1981, the original recipes for Butterfinger and Baby Ruth were lost. Nabisco had to re-create the candy bars from scratch.

Serving
Suggestions: Serve these candies on Halloween, along with **coconut-and-almond candy** and **peanut-butter cups**. Cover them with festive foil wrappers or place them in individual candy cups.

Candy-Making
Notes:

Like all brittles, this candy is best made on a dry day. Humidity can make it too sticky and chewy. For pure peanutty goodness, omit the chocolate coating.

Recipe:

1 cup sugar
¹/₃ cup light corn syrup
¹/₃ cup water
1 cup creamy peanut butter
12 ounces semisweet or coating chocolate

1. **Line an 8-by-8-inch pan with foil and butter well.**

2. **Combine sugar, corn syrup, water, and salt in a saucepan. Cook over medium heat until it reaches a boil. Continue cooking until the mixture reaches 300°F, hard crack stage.**

3. **Remove from heat and stir in the peanut butter with a wooden spoon.**

4. **Pour the mixture into the prepared pan.**

5. **Score the candy into 1- by 2-inch pieces with a well-oiled chef's knife.**

6. **Let the candy cool and set, about 1¹/₂ hours. Cut it into pieces.**

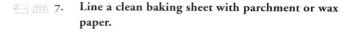 7. **Line a clean baking sheet with parchment or wax paper.**

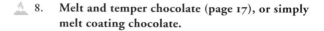 8. **Melt and temper chocolate (page 17), or simply melt coating chocolate.**

9. **Dip the candy centers into the chocolate and place them on the baking sheet to set.**

Yield: About 48 candies

Storage: Store in an airtight container between sheets of wax paper for up to two weeks.

86. **PEANUT-BUTTER CUPS**

General Description: *A thin, slightly soft chocolate shell covers a smooth, creamy peanut butter center, creating a perfect balance of salty and sweet.* The best-known peanut-butter cups are made by Reese's in an iconic round, tapered cup shape with fluted sides.

History: Reese's Peanut Butter Cups were created in 1928 by Harry Burnett Reese, who had formerly worked for Milton Hershey. Although Reese's made several other kinds of candy, the peanut-butter cups in their distinctive brown, orange, and yellow wrapping remain popular today.

Serving Suggestions:	Wrap peanut-butter cups in gold foil and serve them in the Halloween candy bowl. Or pack them in boxed lunches for a special treat.

Candy-Making Notes:	Use a fluted cup mold or a mini muffin tin lined with fluted candy cups.

Recipe:

1 pound milk chocolate
1 cup creamy peanut butter
¹/₃ cup confectioners' sugar
¹/₄ teaspoon salt

1. **Melt and temper the milk chocolate (page 17).**

2. **Use a small spoon or pastry brush to coat the cup molds with tempered chocolate.**

3. **Refrigerate for about 30 minutes to let the chocolate set.**

4. **Combine peanut butter, confectioner's sugar, and salt in a bowl. Spoon the mixture into a pastry bag fitted with a round tip.**

5. **Pipe the peanut butter mixture into the cups, filling to just below the top of the cups.**

6. **Cover the peanut butter mixture with the remaining tempered chocolate. Use an offset spatula to smooth the tops.**

7. **Refrigerate peanut-butter cups until set (about 1 hour) before removing them from molds.**

Yield: About 48 peanut-butter cups

Storage: Store in an airtight container in a cool, dry place for up to 1 week.

87. **PEANUT PATTIES**

General Description: *This unusual candy features peanuts covered in a sweet, gooey, fudge-like mixture that is tinted red and formed into a disk.* Peanut patties are a regional favorite in Texas, where they are typically found wrapped in plastic and sold at local convenience stores. They are prized for their vivid red color and supremely sweet flavor. Sometimes they are called *peanut rounders*, but they can be formed into other shapes as well. Texan peanut patties are often shaped like the state.

History: Peanut patties are found almost exclusively in the American South, especially Texas and Oklahoma, where peanuts are a common crop. One of the best-known brands of peanut patties is Goodart's, which started producing the candy in 1939.

Serving Suggestions:

These patties are typically tinted red or pink. Use greased cookie cutters to form the candy mixture into different shapes in step 6.

Candy-Making Notes:

The most common peanuts used in candy are Spanish peanuts, which have a rich, robust flavor. Like **fudge**, this candy needs to be beaten until it turns smooth and thick for a creamy, soft texture.

Recipe:

2 cups sugar
¹/₂ cup corn syrup
1 cup whole milk
¹/₈ teaspoon salt
2 cups raw peanuts
4 tablespoons unsalted butter, room temperature
1 teaspoon vanilla extract
Few drops red food coloring

1. **Line a baking sheet with parchment paper or a silicone baking mat.**

2. **Combine sugar, corn syrup, milk, and salt in a saucepan. Bring to a boil over medium heat.**

3. **Stir in peanuts. Continue cooking until the mixture reaches 248°F, soft ball stage.**

4. **Remove from heat and add the butter. Stir until butter is fully incorporated. Stir in vanilla and food coloring.**

5. **Beat the mixture vigorously with a wooden spoon until thick and creamy, about 5 minutes.**

6. **Drop spoonfuls of the mixture onto the baking sheet to form 4-inch round patties. Let set at room temperature before serving.**

Yield: About 10 peanut patties

Storage: Store in an airtight container between sheets of wax paper for up to 2 weeks.

88. **RUM BALLS**

General Description: *Rich, sweet, and just a little naughty, rum balls are a cherished tradition at many family holiday gatherings.* These round candies are made from a jumble of cookie crumbs, ground nuts, and confectioners' sugar bound together with honey and a healthy dose of rum. The result is dense, moist, and intense—almost truffle-like.

History: Rum balls are a favorite in North America and Australia. Bourbon balls are a version that is especially popular in the American South. Many versions exist because the simplicity of the recipe makes it easy to adapt.

Serving
Suggestions:

Rum balls are so easy to make that they are a great last-minute party favor. You can make alcohol-free versions for children: Substitute orange juice for the rum.

Candy-Making
Notes:

Try other nuts—such as walnuts or almonds—instead of pecans. Replace the vanilla wafers with graham crackers, shortbread, or other cookies. Instead of rolling rum balls in confectioners' sugar, you can coat them in granulated sugar, shredded coconut, or sprinkles.

Recipe:

1 cup pecans, toasted and finely chopped
1¹/₂ cups vanilla wafer cookies, finely crushed
³/₄ cup confectioners' sugar
2 tablespoons cocoa powder
2 tablespoons honey
¹/₄ cup rum
¹/₂ cup confectioners' sugar for rolling

1. **Combine pecans, vanilla cookie crumbs, confectioners' sugar, and cocoa powder in a large bowl.**

2. **Add honey and rum and stir to combine.**

3. **Form the mixture into 1¹/₂-inch balls with your hands, and roll them in confectioners' sugar.**

4. **If possible, refrigerate 24 hours before serving.**

Yield: About 48 rum balls

Storage: Store in an airtight container in the refrigerator for up to 1 week. The flavor improves over time.

89. 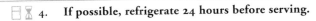 **SOUTHERN PECAN PRALINES**

General Description: *These creamy, gooey disks of brown sugar are studded with pecans.* Unlike **French praline** recipes, Southern praline recipes call for pecans, and the sugar coating is made with brown sugar and cream for a rich, thick candy coating.

History: Southern pecan pralines are a direct descendant of **French pralines**. The confection travelled across the Atlantic to the French colony of New Orleans in the late 1700s. Recipes for pralines were adapted to use the local pecans, and Southern pecan praline recipes began appearing in American cookbooks by the 1760s. In the early 1800s, free black women who sold homemade pralines in the French Quarter became known as *pralinières*. Today, Southern pecan pralines are a classic American candy and a particular favorite in Louisiana, Georgia, and Texas.

Serving Suggestions:	Use pralines in your other desserts: Top an ice cream sundae with pralines or grind the disks and use the powder as a topping or crunchy layer in a cake.
Candy-Making Notes:	Praline recipes have always been fiercely guarded family secrets, so no two are alike. You can take the liberty of modifying this one by using different nuts or adding a dash of bourbon or rum. For an even nuttier flavor, toast the pecans before adding them into the mixture in step 4.
Recipe:	**1 cup light brown sugar** **1 cup sugar** **1 cup heavy cream** **4 tablespoons unsalted butter** **¹/4 teaspoon salt** **2 cups chopped pecans** **1 teaspoon vanilla extract**

1. **Line several baking sheets with parchment paper or silicone baking mats.**

2. **Combine the sugars, cream, butter, and salt in a saucepan. Cook over medium heat, stirring constantly until it reaches a boil.**

3. **Continue cooking, without stirring, until the mixture reaches 236°F, soft ball stage.**

4. **Remove from the heat and add the pecans and vanilla. Stir with a wooden spoon until thick and creamy.**

5. **Drop spoonfuls of the mixture onto baking sheets. Let cool and harden.**

Yield: About 45 pralines

Storage: Store in an airtight container between layers of wax paper for up to 1 week.

90. **TURTLE CANDY**

General Description: *Turtle candy is a classic American confection made of caramel and chocolate poured over four or five pecan halves that are arranged to look like the head and feet of a turtle.* It is one of the easiest candies to make at home: You can use the recipe on pages 254–55 or simply pour melted chocolate over store-bought caramels and nuts.

History: Turtle candies were first made in 1920 in Chicago by the candy company Rowntree DeMet's. Because of the candy, the flavor combination of chocolate, caramel, and pecans has also become known as *turtle*, as in turtle bars, turtle sundaes, and turtle brownies.

Serving
Suggestions:

Boxes and tins of turtle candy are a popular holiday gift. They can also be used to decorate cakes or served with ice cream.

Candy-Making
Notes:

You can use store-bought soft caramels instead of making the caramel in steps 2, 3, and 4. Simply place the caramels on top of each pecan cluster and heat them in a 300°F oven for 5 minutes or until the caramels have softened and melted over the pecans.

Recipe:

3 cups whole pecan halves
2 cups light brown sugar
1 cup unsalted butter
1 cup light corn syrup
1/8 teaspoon salt
1 can (14 ounces) sweetened condensed milk
1 teaspoon vanilla extract
8 ounces semisweet chocolate

1. **Line several baking sheets with parchment paper or silicone baking mats. Arrange the pecan halves on the sheets, using 4 or 5 halves to form a turtle shape if desired.**

2. **Combine the sugar, brown sugar, corn syrup, and salt in a large saucepan. Cook over medium heat until it reaches a boil.**

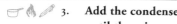 3. **Add the condensed milk and continue cooking until the mixture reaches 248°F, firm ball stage.**

4. **Remove from heat and stir in the vanilla extract.**

5. **Drop spoonfuls of caramel onto the pecan clusters.**

6. **Refrigerate the candies about 15 minutes or until the caramel has set. Melt the chocolate.**

7. **Dip the turtles in the chocolate. Place them on baking sheets to set.**

Yield: About 40 turtles

Storage: Store in an airtight container between sheets of wax paper for up to 2 weeks.

Fun and Simple Classics

91. **CANDIED FLOWERS**

General
Description:

Candied flowers are fresh flower petals or whole blossoms that have been coated in egg white and dipped in sugar. After setting, the coating preserves the flower and adds extra sweetness and crunch. Some recipes for candying flowers involve submersing them in sugar syrup, like **candied fruit**.

History:

People have eaten flowers since ancient times. Myriad varieties, from jasmine to chrysanthemum to chamomile, have been brewed into tea, added to salads, and used to flavor everything from jams to ice creams. Recipes for candying flowers were recorded as early as the 1600s in England. The idea may have come from a desire to preserve blooms and turn attractive flowers into a charming confection.

Serving
Suggestions:

Candied flowers can be eaten out of hand or used to decorate cakes, cupcakes, and other desserts. They are a beautiful decoration for **dipped truffles** and other chocolates.

Candy-Making
Notes:

Make sure that the flowers you choose are edible and organic. Some flowers are poisonous and should not be used. Common edible flowers that candy well are roses, violets, daisies, apple blossoms, nasturtiums, and lilacs.

Recipe: **About 20 flower blossoms**
           2 egg whites
           1 cup superfine sugar

1.   **Ensure the flowers are clean, dry, and free of blemishes.**

2.   **Place egg whites into a small bowl and whisk until frothy. Place the sugar in a separate small bowl.**

3.   **Using a pastry brush or small artist's brush, coat a flower with egg white, covering all the petals evenly.**

4.   **Dip the flower into the sugar and gently shake it to get rid of any excess sugar.**

5.   **Place the flower on a wire rack to dry. Finish the rest of the flowers the same way.**

Yield: About 20 candied flowers

Storage: Store in an airtight container for up to 1 month.

92. 📷   **CANDIED NUTS**

General
Description:
A sweet and sometimes spicy sugar coating turns nuts into toothsome finger food. Some are glazed with hot sugar syrup, whereas others are coated with a sugar mixture and baked. Most recipes call for a pinch of spice such as cinnamon or nutmeg, but more intense spices, such as cayenne, have also become popular.

History:
Candied nuts are descended from **pralines**. French confectioners use them to decorate desserts or grind them to make nutty fillings for cakes and chocolates. In North America, candied nuts are touted as a simple snack for even the most inexperienced cook.

Serving
Suggestions:
Once you have candied nuts, you'll never put out a can of salted peanuts for guests again. Experiment with spices like nutmeg, ginger, or chili powder.

Candy-Making
Notes:
Almost any nut can be candied, but the most common ones are almonds, peanuts, pecans, and walnuts.

Recipe:
2 egg whites
1/2 cup sugar
1/4 cup light brown sugar
3/4 teaspoon ground cinnamon
1/2 teaspoon salt
2 cups pecan halves

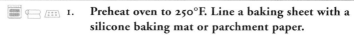 1. **Preheat oven to 250°F. Line a baking sheet with a silicone baking mat or parchment paper.**

2. **In a bowl, whisk the egg whites with a tablespoon of water until frothy.**

3. **Combine the sugars, cinnamon, and salt in another bowl.**

4. **Add pecans to egg whites and stir to coat evenly. Toss them in the sugar mixture until completely coated. Spread out the nuts onto the prepared baking sheet.**

5. **Bake for 45 minutes, shaking the sheet and stirring the nuts every 15 minutes.**

Yield: About 2 cups of candied nuts

Storage: Store in an airtight container for up to 1 month.

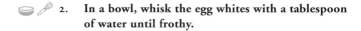

93. **CARAMEL CORN**

General
Description: *What better way to turn a favorite salty snack into a candy than by adding caramel?* Caramel corn is classic popcorn coated in sweet caramel or molasses for a sticky-sweet treat. It comes in loose, freeform clusters or balls held together by the caramel. At

Christmastime it is packed into decorative tins and given as gifts.

History:

Cracker Jack, a commercial version of caramel corn made with popcorn and peanuts coated in molasses, was invented by the Rueckheim brothers in 1893. The term *cracker jack* was coined around the same time as slang for a person of excellence or great ability.

Serving
Suggestions:

You can add a little more salt to give caramel corn a real sweet-and-salty flavor. Or add a ½ teaspoon of cinnamon, nutmeg, or even chili pepper.

Candy-Making
Notes:

You can use microwaved or homemade popcorn for this recipe.

Recipe:

12 cups popped corn
1½ cups sugar
½ cup dark brown sugar
½ cup light corn syrup
½ cup butter
½ teaspoon salt
½ teaspoon baking soda
1 cup salted peanuts, optional

1. **Place popcorn into a large bowl or baking pan.**

2. **Combine sugar, brown sugar, corn syrup, butter, and salt in a saucepan and bring to a boil over**

medium heat.

 3. **Continue cooking the mixture until it reaches 250°F, or hard crack stage.**

4. **Remove from heat and stir in the baking soda. The mixture will foam slightly.**

5. **Pour mixture over the popcorn and stir.**

6. **Add nuts if desired and stir to combine.**

7. **Spread caramel corn on a baking sheet to dry and then break it into clumps, or form it into balls with your hands and then place it on a baking sheet to dry.**

Yield: About 12 cups caramel corn

Storage: Store in an airtight container for up to 3 weeks.

 ## CEREAL CANDY

General Description:
Crunchy breakfast cereal is covered in a buttery, vanilla-scented sugar syrup and poured into a pan to harden. The resulting clusters are like a sweet version of trail mix, terrifically crisp and good for snacking. Almost any sugary breakfast cereal can be used, making this

candy more versatile than **crisped rice treats** and a delicious way to use up nearly empty boxes of cereal.

History:

Dry breakfast cereals were invented in America in the 1860s as a health food for hospital patients, replacing the traditional heavy breakfast of sausages and eggs. In the 1930s, housewives discovered that they can be useful cooking ingredients, adding quick crunch and flavor to recipes. Sweet, crisp breakfast cereals quickly became an invaluable addition to baked sweets such as **crisped rice treats**.

Serving Suggestions:

Cereal candy is ideal for snacking, packing in lunches, or taking along on hikes. You can also form the mixture into balls like **caramel corn**, and top them with ribbons for edible table decorations at children's birthday parties.

Candy-Making Notes:

Feel free to use a combination of cereals for a variety of tastes and textures.

Recipe:

8 cups cereal
1 cup sugar
²/₃ cup light corn syrup
¹/₂ cup unsalted butter
1 teaspoon vanilla extract

1. **Line a baking sheet with wax paper or a silicone baking mat.**

2. **Place cereal in a large bowl and set aside.**

3. **Combine sugar, corn syrup, and butter in a sauce-pan and bring to a boil over medium heat, stirring occasionally.**

4. **Continue cooking until the mixture reaches 230°F, soft ball stage.**

5. **Remove from heat and stir in vanilla.**

6. **Pour mixture over the cereal and stir to coat.**

7. **Turn out mixture onto the baking sheet and spread it into an even layer with a rubber spatula. Let it cool and set for 1 hour before breaking into pieces.**

Yield: About 50 pieces

Storage: Keep in an airtight container at room temperature for up to 2 weeks.

Variation: ***Peanut-Butter Cereal Candy***
A very popular addition to cereal candy is peanut butter, which makes it an even stickier, gooier treat.

7 cups cereal
1/2 cup Spanish peanuts
1 cup sugar

1 cup light corn syrup
1 cup creamy peanut butter
1 teaspoon vanilla extract

1. Line a baking sheet with wax paper or a silicone baking mat.

2. Combine cereal and peanuts in a large bowl and set aside.

3. Combine sugar and corn syrup in a saucepan and bring to a boil over medium heat, stirring occasionally.

5. Remove from heat and add peanut butter. Stir vigorously with a wooden spoon until fully combined. Add in vanilla and stir to combine.

6. Pour peanut butter mixture over the cereal mixture and stir to coat.

7. Turn out mixture onto the baking sheet and spread it into an even layer with a rubber spatula. Let it cool and set for 1 hour before breaking into pieces.

95. **CHOCOLATE-COVERED COFFEE BEANS**

General
Description:

Dipped in melted chocolate, coffee beans become a doubly addictive candy. The lush sweetness of dark chocolate makes the bitterness of the coffee bean easier on the palate. Chocolate-covered coffee beans are naturally found in coffee shops.

History:

Chocolate-covered coffee beans are a type of **dragée**, since they are made by a similar process as **Jordan almonds** and other coated nuts. Kopper's Chocolate, a New York candy company, is credited with coming up with the chocolate-covered coffee bean in the 1930s. Sometimes the candy is called *chocolate-covered espresso beans*, which is a misnomer: *Espresso* refers to a specific method of brewing the coffee, so there is no such thing as espresso beans.

Serving
Suggestions:

Package these coffee beans in cellophane bags tied with ribbon for holiday gifts or end-of-party favors for guests to take home.

Candy-Making
Notes:

Use your favorite blend of coffee beans, but be sure they are roasted, since raw coffee beans taste bitter. Coffee beans contain much more caffeine than brewed coffee, so it's advisable to indulge in no more than a few in one sitting.

Recipe: **1 cup roasted coffee beans**
16 ounces bittersweet chocolate or coating
chocolate

1. **Line a baking sheet with parchment or wax paper.**

2. **Melt and temper the chocolate (page 17), or simply melt the coating chocolate.**

3. **Add beans to the chocolate and stir to coat.**

4. **Remove beans from chocolate, let any excess run off, and place them on the baking sheet to set.**

Yield: About 50 beans

Storage: Store at room temperature for up to 2 weeks. If you used chocolate chips, you may need to refrigerate them.

---

96. **CHOCOLATE-DIPPED POTATO CHIPS**

General
Description: *Decadent chocolate-dipped potato chips are chips—or crisps in the United Kingdom—coated in semisweet chocolate.* They are now sold by several candy companies, but homemade chocolate-dipped potato chips are especially rich, sweet, salty, and crunchy.

History: The French may have invented truffles, but the

Americans have created the ultimate couch potato food. Chocolate-dipped potato chips are a recent invention and part of a trend toward salty-sweet confections such as **fleur de sel caramels**. This novelty snack has become increasingly popular in candy shops, mainly in North America.

Serving Suggestions:
Chocolate-dipped potato chips are a fun party snack year-round. They can be dipped halfway in chocolate or coated completely.

Candy-Making Notes:
Thicker chips work better than thin, breakable ones. Use ruffled or classic cut potato chips.

Recipe:
3 cups potato chips
16 ounces semisweet or coating chocolate

1. **Line a baking sheet with parchment or wax paper.**

2. **Melt and temper the chocolate (page 17), or simply melt the coating chocolate.**

3. **Dip chips in the chocolate.**

4. **Let excess chocolate run off before placing dipped chips on the baking sheet.**

5. **Let chocolate set before serving or dipping in a**

**contrasting chocolate, drizzling with more choco-
late, or serving.**

Yield: About 40 chips

Storage: Store at room temperature for up to 3 days.

---

97. CHOCOLATE-DIPPED PRETZELS

General
Description: *The humble pretzel takes a gourmet turn when deca-
dently dipped in chocolate.* Traditionally-shaped pretzels or pretzel sticks are covered in melted chocolate.
They can be drizzled with additional chocolate or
covered in sprinkles.

History: Pretzels are believed to have been invented by a monk
as treats to reward church-going children; the crossed
arms of the pretzel resemble arms at prayer. Covered
in chocolate, they have become a holiday favorite in
North America, alongside yogurt-dipped pretzels and
chocolate-dipped Oreos.

Serving
Suggestions: Chocolate-dipped pretzels are especially popular at
Christmastime. Dip pretzels in white chocolate and
coat with red and green sprinkles for a festive treat.

Candy-Making
Notes: The thinner, traditionally shaped pretzels work better
than thick pretzels.

Recipe: **3 cups pretzels**
16 ounces semisweet chocolate, or coating chocolate

1. **Line a baking sheet with parchment or wax paper.**

2. **Melt and temper the chocolate (page 17), or simply melt the coating chocolate.**

3. **Place pretzels in the chocolate and stir to coat.**

4. **Let excess chocolate run off before placing dipped pretzels on the baking sheet.**

5. **Let chocolate set before serving, dipping in a contrasting chocolate, or drizzling with more chocolate. Add sprinkles before the chocolate sets.**

Yield: About 40 pretzels

Storage: Store at room temperature for up to 3 days.

98. **CHOCOLATE FONDUE**

General
Description: *Proving the adage that everything is better with chocolate, this fondue is the ultimate do-it-yourself sweet.*
Eating chocolate fondue is a natural party activity that lets eager participants dip fruit, pieces of cake,

and other tidbits into a pot of warm melted chocolate. Fondue parties were in vogue in America during the 1960s and '70s. This surprisingly simple dessert seems to be making a comeback: It's time to dust off the old fondue sets.

History:
The original cheese fondue originated in Switzerland. It was a simple peasant dish that utilized leftover bits of cheese and bread, turning them into a hearty meal. This evolved into more elaborate concoctions that combined cheese, wine, eggs, and spices. Legend has it that chocolate fondue was invented in the 1960s at the Chalet Suisse restaurant in New York City. It was made with Toblerone, the Swiss chocolate bar, which had just been invented. In an attempt to promote this new candy, the restaurant started a sweet fondue fad.

Serving
Suggestions:
Some of the traditional "dippers" for chocolate fondue include strawberries, bananas, and orange slices, marshmallows, small cubes of pound cake or angel food cake, meringues, macaroons, ladyfingers, and biscotti. You can serve several pots of fondue with different kinds of chocolate so guests can compare flavors.

Candy-Making
Notes:
Although a fondue pot is designed to keep fondue warm and present it attractively, it is not necessary to use one. You can simply serve fondue in the same pot you made it in. A heavy, sturdy saucepan is less likely

to burn the chocolate and will retain heat longer. If the fondue starts to cool and set, simply place it back over the stove for a few minutes.

Recipe: **1 cup cream**
12 ounces semisweet chocolate, roughly chopped
1 teaspoon Grand Marnier
Items to dip such as fruit, cake, or cookies, cut in 1-inch pieces
Fondue forks or bamboo skewers

1. **Place cream in a saucepan over medium heat until it starts to boil.**

2. **Add chocolate stir until it is melted. Remove from heat and stir in Grand Marnier.**

3. **Pour fondue into a fondue pot if desired. Serve fondue with dipping items and fondue forks or bamboo skewers.**

Yield: About 2 cups of fondue

Storage: Refrigerate in an airtight container for up to 3 days.

99. **CHOCOLATE PEANUT CLUSTERS**

General
Description:
Chocolate peanut clusters are a simple combination of roasted peanuts and smooth, sweet chocolate. Although most clusters contain just these two elements, the creativity of candy-makers has resulted in clusters with all sorts of goodies embedded in the chocolate. **Turtles** are a form of cluster, as are **rocky road** candies; the irregular, casual appearance of these candies is what defines them.

History:
Although clusters appear similar to French confections **rochers** and **mendiants**, they are probably a North American invention. One of the most well-known commercial forms of this candy is the Goo Goo Cluster, which combines a mound of peanuts, caramel, and marshmallows under a chocolate coating. Invented by the Standard Candy Company in Nashville in 1912, the Goo Goo Cluster is one of the most popular candies in the American South.

Serving
Suggestions:
Chocolate clusters are a great candy to make with leftover ingredients from other baking endeavors. Their homespun appearance makes them an easy treat to whip up for casual get-togethers.

Candy-Making
Notes:
These clusters are one of the simplest candies to make on a whim, given the freeform recipe. You can substitute or add just about any ingredient: other nuts,

dried fruit, coconut, or marshmallows.

Recipe: **12 ounces semisweet chocolate**
1 cup roasted peanuts

1. **Line a baking sheet with parchment paper or a silicone baking mat.**

2. **Melt chocolate in a metal bowl set over a pot of simmering water, stirring occasionally so it will melt evenly.**

3. **Add in the peanuts and stir to coat.**

4. **Drop spoonfuls of the mixture onto the baking sheet. Let set before serving.**

Yield: About 20 clusters

Storage: Store in an airtight container in a cool, dry place for up to 2 weeks.

100. CINNAMON CANDY

General Description: *Hot and spicy instead of sweet, cinnamon candy packs a delightfully piquant punch.* Commercial varieties include the creatively named classic American candies Red Hots, Hot Tamales, and Atomic Fireballs.

History: Cinnamon originated in India and was among the
            highly coveted spices sold along the ancient trade
            routes from Asia to Europe. Cinnamon oil is made
            from the bark and leaves of the cinnamon tree.
            Flavoring extracts can evaporate in the intensely
            hot sugar syrups used in candy making; cinnamon
            oil's potency gives it better flavor retention, which
            is why it was one of the first successful flavorings
            for hard candies.

Serving   With its vibrant red color and stimulating flavor,
Suggestions: cinnamon candy is a natural match for Valentine's
            Day. You can pour the sugar syrup into heart-shaped
            lollipop molds.

Candy-Making Cinnamon oil is not the same as cinnamon extract;
Notes: it is much more potent and should be handled with
            care. You can use cinnamon extract, but the flavor
            will be less strong.

Recipe: **2 cups sugar**
            1 cup light corn syrup
            1 teaspoon cinnamon oil
            1 teaspoon red food coloring

1. **Coat a baking sheet with cooking spray.**

2. **Combine sugar, 1/2 cup water, and corn syrup
    in a saucepan and bring to a boil over high heat.**

3. **Continue cooking without stirring until it reaches 300°F, hard crack stage. Remove from heat.**

 4. **Add the cinnamon oil and red food coloring and stir to combine. Be very careful as the fumes from the oil and hot sugar mixture can be very hot. Do not lean over the saucepan.**

5. **Pour out the mixture onto the baking sheet.**

6. **Let the candy cool and harden. Break into pieces.**

Yield: About 2 cups of cinnamon candy

Storage: Store in a cool, dry place for up to 1 month.

Variation: ***Molded Cinnamon Candies***
Pour the hot candy mixture into molds in step 5. Let it harden before unmolding.

 Storage: Wrap in cellophane that is twist tied shut, and store in a cool dry place for up to 1 month.

---

101. **COCONUT HAYSTACKS**

General
Description: *A mixture of melted chocolate and toasted coconut, these haystacks are pleasantly chewy and filling.* Haystacks can be seen as a simple version of

coconut macaroons; some macaroon recipes are even called *haystack cookies.*

History:

Coconut haystacks are an American tradition. Recipes for coconut haystacks were commonly found in cookbooks in the 1950s. Commercial and homemade versions have spread throughout North America and the United Kingdom.

Serving Suggestions:

You can dress up these haystacks by sprinkling slivered almonds, chocolate chips, or chocolate kisses on top. They are especially popular at picnics and potlucks.

Candy-Making Notes:

Stir the toasting coconut periodically; it can burn very quickly, and the bits at the edges invariably brown faster than the center.

Recipe:

2 cups sweetened flaked coconut
8 ounces semisweet chocolate, chopped
Extra coconut for sprinkling

1. **Preheat oven to 350°F. Line a baking sheet with parchment or wax paper.**

2. **Spread coconut on a clean baking sheet. Toast in the oven for 5 to 8 minutes until golden brown.**

3. **Melt chocolate in a metal bowl set over a pot of**

simmering water, stirring occasionally.

4. **Add the toasted coconut and stir to combine.**

5. **Drop rounded tablespoons of the mixture onto the lined baking sheet, forming haystack-like mounds. Sprinkle untoasted coconut over the tops.**

6. **Chill in refrigerator for about 1 hour until firm.**

Yield: About 16 haystacks

Storage: Refrigerate in an airtight container for up to 2 weeks.

102. **COW PATTIES**

General Description: *These colorfully named candies are also known by a more appetizing name:* no-bake peanut butter chocolate cookies. A happy jumble of oats, peanut butter, and cocoa powder held together by a buttery sugar syrup, these confections have a rather down-to-earth appearance. However, their ease of creation is only matched by the speed at which they disappear from the table.

History: Cow patties are on the line between cookie and candy. The recipe requires cooking sugar, which is part of candy making, but the flat, roundish form of the final product is definitely cookie-like. The concept of "no-bake" cookies has also helped to blur the line between cookies and candy, since most traditional cookies require baking, but candies do not. This ambiguity has led to other sweet treats such as **rum balls** or **crisped rice treats** being labeled as cookies or candy in different cookbooks.

Serving Suggestions:
❈ ☀ ♧ ❄

You can serve cow patties on a cookie plate with chocolate chip and oatmeal raisin cookies or in a candy bowl with **no-fail fudge** and **no-cook fondant** creams.

Candy-Making Notes:

The key to these treats is making sure the sugar is fully melted and the syrup is smooth.

Recipe:

2 cups sugar
$^1/_3$ cup unsalted butter
$^1/_2$ cup milk
3 tablespoons cocoa powder
$^1/_2$ cup peanut butter
1 teaspoon vanilla extract
2$^1/_2$ cups rolled oats

1. **Line a baking sheet with wax paper or a silicone baking mat.**

2. **Combine sugar, butter, milk, and cocoa powder in a saucepan. Bring to a boil over medium heat, stirring occasionally to ensure that the sugar is fully melted. Remove from heat.**

3.   **Stir in the peanut butter and vanilla.**

4.   **Add the oats and stir until they are fully distributed throughout the mixture.**

5.   **Drop mounds of the mixture onto the baking sheet, forming 3-inch round patties. Let them set for about 1 hour before serving.**

Yield: About 15 patties

Storage: Store in an airtight container for up to 1 week.

103.   **CRISPED RICE TREATS**

General
Description: *These candy bars combine puffed, crispy rice cereal with melted butter and marshmallows for a sticky-sweet treat.* Much of the appeal of these bars comes from their ease of creation and their crispy yet gooey texture. Undoubtedly the most well-known form of this sweet is Kellogg's Rice Krispies Treats, made from their Rice Krispies cereal. However, it is possible to make these bars from any puffed grain cereal.

History: Sweets made of puffed grains mixed with molasses or honey were first made in America in the 19th century and called *popcorn balls* whether or not they contained popcorn. Recipes for puffed rice bars appeared in cookbooks in the early 1930s. Rice Krispies Treats were created in 1939 by Mildred Day, a Kellogg's employee, for a Campfire Girls fundraiser. The recipe proved so popular that Kellogg's began printing it on cereal boxes in 1941. In 1995, Kellogg's began selling premade Rice Krispies Treats, a sign of America's enduring love for this sweet.

Serving
Suggestions:
❁ ☀ ❀ ❄

Crisped rice treats are a great spur-of-the-moment confection because of the few ingredients and quick assembly. Let children add in chocolate chips or colorful sprinkles of their choice. They can also form the rice mixture into shapes by hand or with cookie cutters.

Candy-Making
Notes:

Although these treats are not difficult to remove from the pan, lining it with a sheet of parchment will ensure that the entire piece comes out in one go.

Recipe:

3 tablespoons unsalted butter
10 ounces (4 cups) store-bought marshmallows
6 cups puffed rice cereal

 1.

Line a 13-by-9-by-2-inch baking pan with parchment paper and grease with butter.

2.

Melt butter in a saucepan over low heat. Add marshmallows and stir until completely melted. Remove from heat.

3. **Add cereal to the mixture and stir until well coated.**

4. **Turn out mixture into prepared pan. Use a rubber spatula to spread it evenly.**

5. **Let cool. Remove from pan and cut into squares or use cookie cutters to make shapes.**

Yield: About 24 squares

Storage: Store in an airtight container for up to 1 week.

104. **DATE-NUT ROLL**

General Description: *This old-fashioned, deliciously sweet confection is a classic American homemade candy.* The date-nut roll, also called a *date roll* or *date loaf*, is a soft, chewy sweet made of dates, sugar, and pecans. Most recipes for this candy call for rolling up the candy in a tea towel and storing it in the refrigerator, a charming reminder of the days before plastic wrap and aluminum foil.

History: Dates are naturally sweet fruits that have been enjoyed since the dawn of civilization. They are used in confections such as **sugarplums** and **stuffed dates**. Date-nut rolls are a distinctly American creation. Most date-nut roll recipes are treasured family secrets passed from generation to generation.

Serving Suggestions:	Keep the date-nut roll wrapped in a damp tea towel in the back of the refrigerator, and slice off a few pieces at a time to savor.
Candy-Making Notes:	If you have trouble forming the roll on the towel, lay a piece of wax paper on top of the towel and form the mixture there.
Recipe:	1¹/₂ cups sugar ¹/₂ cup light brown sugar 1 cup milk 1 tablespoon unsalted butter 1 cup (8 ounces) chopped, pitted dates 1 cup chopped pecans 1 teaspoon vanilla extract

 1. **Combine sugars, milk, and butter in a saucepan. Cook over medium heat, stirring occasionally, until the mixture reaches a boil.**

2. **Continue cooking until the mixture reaches 236°F, soft ball stage.**

3. **Remove from heat. Beat mixture with a wooden spoon until it becomes thick and creamy.**

4. **Stir in the dates, nuts, and vanilla extract.**

5. **Dampen a small, clean, cotton towel and spread it on the counter. When the mixture is cool enough to handle, put it on the towel and form it into a log.**

🗄️⏳ 6. **Wrap the log in the towel and refrigerate overnight to let it firm up.**

Yield: About 30 slices

🗄️ Storage: Date-nut rolls are traditionally rolled in a tea towel and refrigerated. They can be stored for up to 1 week wrapped in the towel, or 2 weeks rolled in plastic wrap.

105. 📷 **EASTER EGG NESTS**

General Description: *These charming little nests look so close to the real thing that a bird might mistake one for his home.* However, the materials for these nests—dry chow mein noodles and melted chocolate—are far more tasty than twigs and grass. Crispy chow mein noodles are an unconventional candy-making ingredient, but mixed with chocolate they provide a crunchy, salty-sweet taste like **chocolate-dipped pretzels**. These nests are the perfect container for other Easter treats, such as chocolate eggs or jelly beans.

History: Chow mein is a traditional dish in China. In North America, inventive home cooks have found other uses for these packages of dried noodles. Chow mein noodles can also be mixed with chocolate chips or marshmallows and used to make **cereal candy**.

Serving
Suggestions:

Fill the nests with jellybeans, chocolates, candy eggs, or gumdrops. You can even perch marshmallow chicks inside or sprinkle the nests with colored sprinkles.

Candy-Making
Notes:

The kind of chow mein noodles that works best in this recipe is the La Choy brand that comes in a can. The pieces are pre-cooked, short, and slightly curled, which increases the candy's resemblance to a real bird's nest. If you can't find them, any pre-cooked chow mein noodles will work.

Recipe:

**10 ounces semisweet chocolate
2 cups dry cooked chow mein noodles**

1. **Line a baking sheet with wax paper or a silicone baking mat.**

2. **Melt the chocolate in a metal bowl over a pot of simmering water, stirring occasionally. Remove from heat.**

3. **Fold in the chow mein noodles with a rubber spatula.**

4. **Spoon out 5-inch mounds of noodles onto the**

⏳ **5.**

baking sheet. Use your hands to form the mounds into a nest shape, with an indentation in the center.

Let set for about 1 hour.

Yield: About 12 nests

🍞 Storage: Store in an airtight container for up to 2 weeks.

---

106. 📷 **IRISH POTATO CANDY**

General Description: *Irish potato candies do not contain any potatoes, but they do mimic their appearance.* A mixture of butter, cream cheese, and coconut is formed into balls and then rolled in cinnamon to look like miniature potatoes. They are made in great quantities for St. Patrick's Day in Philadelphia, where they were invented.

History: Irish potato candy is not from Ireland. Cream cheese and coconut weren't common foods in Ireland until the 1900s. It is likely that Philadelphia's large Irish immigrant population invented Irish potato candy.

Serving Suggestions: 🌿 ☀ ☁ ❄ This is an easy, fun candy to make with kids on St. Patrick's Day. Substitute cocoa powder for the cinnamon to make chocolate spuds.

Candy-Making Notes:	The butter and cream cheese need to be about the same temperature in order to combine well.

Recipe:

¹/₄ cup unsalted butter, room temperature
4 ounces cream cheese, room temperature
1 teaspoon vanilla extract
16 ounces confectioners' sugar
2¹/₂ cups sweetened flaked coconut
Ground cinnamon for rolling

1. **In a stand mixer with the paddle attachment, cream the butter and cream cheese on medium speed.**

2. **Add the vanilla and beat to combine.**

3. **Add the confectioners' sugar and beat on low speed until fully incorporated.**

4. **Add the coconut and beat until fully incorporated.**

5. **Form the dough into rough ovals. Roll them in cinnamon and refrigerate until firm before serving.**

Yield: About 50 candies

Storage: Refrigerate in an airtight container for up to 2 weeks.

107. **KETTLE CORN**

General
Description:

This sweet and salty version of caramel corn is a perennial carnival favorite. The corn is popped with a bit of sugar, which caramelizes slightly to give the popcorn a light, sweet glaze.

History:

Kettle corn can be traced back to colonial times. It was first made by German settlers in Pennsylvania in the 1700s. They popped corn kernels in large iron kettles and added a little sugar or honey to the popping corn to sweeten the treat. Kettle corn faded from popularity in the 1900s when it was eclipsed by **caramel corn**, but recently it has made a comeback at carnivals and fairs.

Serving
Suggestions:

Kettle corn is an ideal treat to make for children's parties or summer barbecues. You can add more sugar to your taste, or a pinch of cinnamon or chili powder for a spicy variation.

Candy-Making
Notes:

Use an oil with a high smoking point, such as canola, corn, or peanut. When the oil is hot enough, drop in a few kernels to see if they pop. If they do, pour in the rest of the kernels to cover the bottom of the pot in an even layer. Shake the pot as the kernels pop to prevent burning.

Recipe: **¹/₄ cup canola oil**
            ¹/₂ cup un-popped popcorn
            ¹/₄ cup sugar
            ¹/₄ teaspoon salt

🔥 1.   **Pour oil into a large metal pot that has a handle
        and tight-fitting lid. Cook over medium heat until
        the oil becomes hot.**

🔥 2.   **Add the popcorn and cover it with the lid. Heat
        until the popcorn begins to pop, about 1 to 2 min-
        utes. Remove the lid and add the sugar and salt.
        Replace the lid and continue cooking, shaking the
        pot constantly to ensure that the popcorn does not
        burn. Open the lid slightly to let steam escape.**

🥣 3.   **Once the popping has slowed down, remove pot
        from heat and pour popcorn into a bowl.**

Yield: About 3 cups kettle corn

Storage: Popcorn is best eaten fresh, but you can store in an
            airtight container for up to 3 days.

108a–b. 📷   **NO-COOK FONDANT**

General   *For **fondant** with less fuss, this version of the clas-*
Description: *sic candy can be made in minutes.* No-cook fondant

combines confectioners' sugar and butter in slightly different proportions to yield a creamy fondant that is easy to work with. Just like classic **fondant**, this no-cook sweet can be used as the base for a wide array of beautiful and tasty candies.

History:

No-cook fondant is similar to simple buttercream, also known as *American buttercream*. The combination of confectioners' sugar and butter produces a creamy, sweet icing that can be used like the classic buttercreams made with cooked eggs and sugar. With a little less butter, the same mixture of ingredients produces a smooth paste similar to classic **fondant**.

Serving Suggestions:

Lemon-almond bonbons, violet creams, maple-walnut creams, and vanilla opera creams (pages 179–82) can be made with no-cook fondant; add liquid flavorings or food coloring to the mixture in step 1.

Candy-Making Notes:

Try both versions of fondant to see which you prefer; there are differences in texture and taste. Add the confectioners' sugar slowly and make sure it is fully mixed to prevent pockets of unincorporated sugar.

Recipe:

¹/₃ cup unsalted butter, room temperature
1 pound confectioners' sugar, sifted
¹/₄ cup light corn syrup
1 teaspoon vanilla extract
¹/₂ teaspoon salt

1. **In a stand mixer with the paddle attachment, beat the butter and cream until smooth.**

 2. **Add the confectioners' sugar 1 cup at a time. Beat until it forms a smooth dough.**

 3. **Add corn syrup, vanilla, and salt, and beat to combine.**

4. **You can use the fondant now or scrape it into a container for later use.**

Yield: About 4 cups of fondant

Storage: Refrigerate in an airtight container for up to 1 month.

Variations: ***Fondant Cream Mints***
Fondant flavored with peppermint makes a wonderful soft mint; it can also be the center of a delicious **peppermint patty**. Add 2 drops of peppermint oil to the mixture in step 1. Press small balls of the finished mixture and press into candy molds.

Double Chocolate Creams
Mix in 2 ounces of melted chocolate (step 2). Form small balls of fondant, and use a toothpick to dip them into tempered chocolate or chocolate coating.

109. 📷 **NO-FAIL FUDGE**

General
Description:

One of the most reassuringly named candies, no-fail fudge *or* never-fail fudge *is a simple, quick version of* **fudge**. It cannot be certain that this fudge has never, ever failed. But the recipe removes much of the precision required for classic **fudge**, making a rich, toothsome result much easier. Several versions of no-fail fudge exist, most of them containing ingredients such as condensed milk or Marshmallow Fluff, which substitute the creamy texture that comes from beating and cooking classic fudge.

History:

In the early 1900s, the development of ready-made items such as condensed milk and Marshmallow Fluff started a trend of quick, easy recipes that utilized commercial items to simplify the task of cooking. In the 1930s and 1940s, housewives developed "modern" versions of classic dishes, often aided by manufacturers who marketed their newfangled food-stuffs with recipe ideas. Some reinventions bore only a passing resemblance to the original, whereas others became honored substitutes for the real thing.

Serving
Suggestions:
❀ ☼ ♧ ❄

No-fail fudge is a quick fix for fudge cravings. It is also a great way to introduce children to the joys of candy making.

Candy-Making Notes:
This recipe can be made with chocolate chips. Use a bittersweet chocolate if you want a darker, more refined taste.

Recipe:
2¹/₂ cups sugar
6 tablespoons unsalted butter
1 cup evaporated milk
¹/₂ teaspoon salt
7¹/₂ ounces marshmallow cream, such as Marshmallow Fluff
1 teaspoon vanilla extract
16 ounces semisweet chocolate, chopped
1¹/₂ cups chopped walnuts, if desired

1. **Line an 8-by-8-inch pan with foil and butter well.**

2. **Combine sugar, butter, evaporated milk, and salt in a saucepan and bring to a boil over high heat, stirring occasionally.**

3. **Continue cooking, stirring until the mixture reaches 236°F, soft ball stage.**

4. **Remove from heat and add marshmallow cream, vanilla, and chocolate. Stir until ingredients are melted and fully combined. Add the nuts if desired and stir to combine.**

5. **Pour mixture into prepared pan to cool before**

cutting into 1¹/₂-inch squares.

Yield: About 35 squares of fudge

Storage: Store in an airtight container for up to 2 weeks.

110. **NONPAREILS**

General
Description: *Tiny colored sugar balls, sprinkles, jimmies, hundreds-and-thousands, and other small sweet items that decorate cupcakes and cookies are called* nonpareils, *as are the chocolate candies made by covering small discs of chocolate with these little sugar beads.* Each tiny nonpareil is made by coating an individual sugar crystal in syrup; if the coating process continues, it makes a gobstopper. Nonpareil candies or *button candies* are bite-size chocolate drops coated with these white or rainbow-colored sugar sprinkles. Their distinct candy-coated, chocolatey crunch may be the reason why Sno-Caps have been a favorite among movie-goers for more than 50 years.

History: The French word *nonpareil* means "without equal." French confectioners may have given this name to the candy to signify its invaluable role in decorating cakes and other desserts.

Serving
Suggestions:

Serve nonpareils in the candy dish year-round, wrap them in gift boxes for the holidays, sprinkle them over ice cream, or use them as shingles on gingerbread houses. Although white sugar beads are most commonly used for nonpareils, multicolored beads can be used to match a party theme.

Candy-Making
Notes:

It can be tricky to spoon the chocolate in a consistent size and shape. Round, disc-shaped candy molds make the process easier.

Recipe:

8 ounces bittersweet or coating chocolate
¹/₄ cup nonpareils

1. **Line a baking sheet with parchment paper or a silicone baking mat.**

2. **Melt and temper the chocolate (page 17), or simply melt the coating chocolate.**

3. **Spoon nickel-size circles of tempered chocolate onto the lined baking sheet. Let it set for 2 minutes, then sprinkle sugar beads over the top.**

4. **Let set for 30 minutes or until firm before serving.**

Yield:

About 40 candies

Storage: Store in an airtight container at room temperature for up to 1 month.

111a–b. **PEANUT-BUTTER BALLS**

General
Description: *Peanut-butter balls are the perfect candy for anyone who longs to eat peanut butter straight from the jar.* These treats are little more than balls of peanut butter dipped in melted dark chocolate—pure peanutty goodness. Because they are so simple to make, peanut butter balls are a great choice for beginning candy makers.

History: Peanuts and peanut butter have a unique place in American history. The modern American version of peanut butter was invented in 1895 by John Kellogg, who intended it as a health food for patients. By the 1920s, peanut butter was on its way to becoming an essential part of America's food culture. Peanut-butter balls were likely invented as a simple way to enjoy peanut butter as candy.

Serving
Suggestions: Roll peanut-butter balls in sprinkles or miniature chocolate chips. For a regional variation, make buckeyes (page 297).

Candy-Making
Notes: You can use a toothpick to dip the balls in chocolate; simply smooth over the hole once you have placed the dipped ball back on the baking sheet.

Recipe: 1 cup peanut butter
            $^1/_2$ cup unsalted butter, room temperature
            1 teaspoon vanilla extract
            $^1/_2$ teaspoon salt
            3 cups confectioners' sugar
            8 ounces bittersweet or coating chocolate

1. Line a baking sheet with parchment paper or a silicone baking mat.

2. In a stand mixer, beat peanut butter, butter, vanilla extract, and salt together on medium speed.

3. Add the confectioners' sugar, $^1/_2$ cup at a time, until the mixture is very smooth and firm.

4. Form 1-inch balls and place them on the baking sheet. Refrigerate for 30 minutes or until firm.

5. Melt and temper the chocolate (page 17), or simply melt the coating chocolate.

6. Dip peanut-butter balls in the chocolate and place them back on the baking sheet. Let them set for at least 1 hour before serving.

Yield: About 24 peanut-butter balls

Storage: Refrigerate in an airtight container for up to 1 week.

Variation: **Buckeyes**

In Ohio—also known as the "Buckeye State"—peanut butter balls are left partially un-dipped so that they resemble buckeye nuts.

112a–b. 📷 **POTATO PINWHEELS**

General Description: *Potatoes are an unlikely ingredient for candy, but these potato pinwheels prove the versatility of the spud.* The creamy texture of mashed potatoes makes them a great base for soft candy, and their mild taste easily adapts to added flavors. The mashed potato is combined with confectioners' sugar to create a sweet dough, which is spread with peanut butter and rolled up into a luscious pinwheel.

History: Potato candy was most popular in Northeast America and Canada during the early 1900s. The humble ingredients and easy recipe indicate that it may have been developed to use up leftover mashed potatoes. Cookbooks often call potato pinwheels *after-dinner candy*.

Serving Suggestions: ❀ ☀ ❁ ❄ Make pinwheels with leftover mashed potatoes that aren't seasoned. A common variation is to add 1 cup sweetened shredded coconut to the potato dough. Serve pinwheels at picnics and holiday gatherings.

Candy-Making Notes:	When you add the confectioners' sugar to the potato, it may appear to liquefy. Keep mixing and the dough will come together. Add more confectioners' sugar if it seems too soft or is difficult to roll out.

Recipe:

1 small potato (about 5 ounces), cooked, peeled, and cut into pieces
1 teaspoon vanilla extract
1 pound confectioners' sugar, sifted
1 cup creamy peanut butter

1. **Using a stand mixer or food processor, combine the potato pieces until thoroughly mashed.**

2. **Add vanilla extract and mix to combine.**

3. **Add confectioners' sugar, 1 cup at a time, mixing after each addition.**

4. **Turn out dough onto a piece of plastic wrap. Press it into a flat disk, wrap the plastic wrap around it tightly, and refrigerate for 1 hour or until firm.**

5. **Place a sheet of wax paper on the counter. Roll out the dough to form a square about 1/4 inch thick. Spread peanut butter on top of the square.**

6. **Using the waxed paper to guide the candy, roll it like a jelly roll. Wrap tightly with plastic wrap and refrigerate overnight.**

7. **Slice into ¹/₂-inch rounds to serve.**

Yield: About 30 pinwheels

Storage: Refrigerate in an airtight container for up to 1 week.

Variation: ***Needhams***
In Maine, local potato candies are called *Needhams*. Add 1 cup shredded coconut to the dough in step 3. Spread the dough on a buttered 9 by 13 inch baking pan. Chill until firm and cut into squares. Melt and temper a pound of bittersweet chocolate (page 17), then dip the squares in the chocolate.

113. **ROCKY ROAD**

General Description: *This classic American candy earned its name from its craggy, bumpy appearance.* Marshmallows and nuts are held together with milk chocolate, creating a gooey, nutty, sweet candy. First created as an ice cream flavor, rocky road was later made into a candy bar and is now a popular dessert flavor. Rocky road candy is common in Britain and Australia, where it may contain dried fruit or shredded coconut.

History: The term *rocky road* was coined by William Dreyer of Dreyer's ice cream in 1929. His partner Joseph Edy invented the marshmallow, walnut, and chocolate confection. However, the flavor was not known as "rocky road" until the Great Depression, when Dreyer renamed the ice cream to give the unhappy populace a boost to their spirits. In 1950, Annabelle Candy Company in San Francisco produced the Rocky Road candy bar that combined chocolate, marshmallows, and cashews.

Serving
Suggestions: Sprinkle pieces of rocky road over ice cream, mix it in to cookie batter, or use it to decorate cakes and cupcakes.

Candy-Making
Notes: The nuts that make rocky road rocky have varied over the years. Substitute pecans, almonds, or other nuts in this recipe.

Recipe: **14 ounces milk chocolate**
3 cups miniature marshmallows
1 cup walnuts, coarsely chopped

1. **Line a 9-by-9-by-2 inch baking pan with foil and butter well.**

2. **Melt chocolate in a metal bowl set over a pot of simmering water, stirring occasionally. Remove from heat as soon as the chocolate is melted.**

3. **Stir in the marshmallows and walnuts. Spread the mixture into the baking pan.**

4. **Refrigerate 30 minutes or until firm. Use a sharp knife to cut into pieces.**

Yield: About 25 pieces

Storage: Store in an airtight container for up to 1 week.

Table of Equivalencies (U.S. to Metric)

Volume

U.S.	Metric
1/4 teaspoon	1.25 milliliters
1/2 teaspoon	2.5 milliliters
1 teaspoon	5 milliliters
1 tablespoon (3 teaspoons)	15 milliliters
1 fluid ounce (2 tablespoons)	30 milliliters
1/4 cup	60 milliliters
1/3 cup	80 milliliters
1/2 cup	120 milliliters
1 cup	240 milliliters
1 pint (2 cups)	480 milliliters
1 quart (2 pints)	960 milliliters
1 gallon (4 quarts)	3.84 liters

Weight

U.S.	Metric
1 ounce	28 grams
4 ounces (1/4 lb)	113 grams
8 ounces (1/2 lb)	227 grams
12 ounces (3/4 lb)	340 grams
16 ounces (1 lb)	454 grams

Formulas

U.S.	Metric
Cups to liters	Multiply cups by 0.236
Cups to milliliters	Multiply cups by 236.59
Inches to centimeters	Multiply inches by 2.54
Ounces to grams	Multiply ounces by 28.35
Ounces to milliliters	Multiply ounces by 29.57
Tablespoons to milliliters	Multiply tablespoons by 14.79
Teaspoons to milliliters	Multiply teaspoons by 4.93

Oven Temperatures

Degrees Fahrenheit	Degrees Centigrade	British Gas Marks
200°F	93°C	—
250°F	120°C	1/4
275°F	140°C	1
300°F	150°C	2
325°F	165°C	3
350°F	175°C	4
375°F	190°C	5
400°F	200°C	6
450°F	230°C	8
500°F	260°C	10

High Altitude Baking Alterations

Feet above sea level	Per teaspoon baking powder	Per cup sugar	Per cup liquid
3,000	–1/8 teaspoon	–1/2 to 1 tablespoon	1 to 2 tablespoons
5,000	–1/8 to –1/4 teaspoon	–1/2 to 2 tablespoons	2 to 4 tablespoons
7,000+	–1/4 teaspoon	–1 to 3 tablespoons	3 to 4 tablespoons

Common Conversions

All-purpose flour		
1 tablespoon	1/4 ounce	7 grams
1 cup	5 ounces	140 grams

Granulated sugar		
1 tablespoon	1/2 ounce	14 grams
1 cup	5 ounces	140 grams

Brown sugar		
1 tablespoon	1/2 ounce	14 grams
1 cup	8 ounces	220 grams

Confectioners' sugar		
1 tablespoon	1/4 ounce	7 grams
1 cup	4 ounces	110 grams

Butter				
1 tablespoon		1/2 ounce		14 grams
1 cup	16 tablespoons	8 ounces	226 grams	2 sticks butter

Milk or heavy cream	
1 cup	8 fluid ounces

Common Substitutions

Ingredient	Amount	Substitute
Baking powder	1 teaspoon	$1/4$ teaspoon baking soda plus $5/8$ teaspoon cream of tartar
Butter	1 cup	1 cup margarine; 1 cup butter substitute; $7/8$ cup vegetable oil
Buttermilk	1 cup	1 cup sour cream; 1 tablespoon lemon juice or white vinegar plus enough milk to equal 1 cup; 1 cup milk plus $13/4$ teaspoons cream of tartar
Corn syrup	1 cup	$11/4$ cups sugar or brown sugar plus an additional $1/4$ cup of a liquid in the recipe
Cornstarch	1 tablespoon	$21/2$ teaspoons potato starch or arrowroot; 5 teaspoons rice starch 2 tablespoons quick-cooking tapioca
Cream	1 cup	$11/2$ tablespoons melted butter plus enough whole milk to equal 1 cup
Egg	1 large egg	$31/2$ room-temperature egg substitute
Granulated sugar	1 cup	$13/4$ cups confectioners' sugar; 1 cup super-fine sugar
Honey	1 cup	$11/4$ cups granulated sugar plus an additional $1/3$ cup of a liquid in the recipe
Lemon juice	1 teaspoon	$1/2$ teaspoon white vinegar or rice vinegar
Light brown sugar	1 cup	$1/2$ cup brown sugar (packed) plus $1/2$ cup granulated sugar
Milk	1 cup	$1/2$ cup evaporated milk plus $1/2$ cup water; 1 cup soy milk or rice milk

Further Reading

Almond, Steve. *Candyfreak*. Chapel Hill: Algonquin Books, 2004.

Benning, Lee Edwards. *Oh, Fudge!* New York: Henry Holt and Company, 1990.

Bloom, Carole. *Truffles, Candies, and Confections*. Berkeley: Ten Speed Press, 2004.

DeGros, J. H. *Candy Cookbook*. New York: Fawcett Publications, 1953.

Greweling, Peter. *Chocolates and Confections*. Hoboken: John Wiley & Sons, 2007.

Mason, Laura. *Sugar-Plums and Sherbet*. Wiltshire: Prospect Books, 2004.

Medrich, Alice. *Bittersweet: Recipes and Tales from a Life in Chocolate*. New York: Artisan, 2003.

Montagne, Prosper, ed. *Larousse Gastronomique*. New York: Clarkson Potter, 2001.

Nichols, Nell. *Homemade Candy*. New York: Doubleday, 1970.

Pappas, Lou Seibert. *The Christmas Candy Book*. San Francisco: Chronicle Books, 2002.

Recchiutti, Michael. *Chocolate Obsession*. New York: Stewart, Tabori, and Chang, 2005.

Scharffenberger, John. *Essence of Chocolate*. New York: Hyperion, 2006.

Sharrock, Jane. *Who Wants Candy?* New York: Berkley Publishing Group, 2004.

Shotts, Andrew Garrison. *Making Artisan Chocolates*. Gloucester: Quarry Books, 2007.

Van Arsdale, May. *Candy Recipes and Other Confections*. New York: Dover, 1975.

Resources

Here are some online sources where you can find many of the tools used for candy making, such as candy thermometers, beautifully designed molds, wrappers, lollipop sticks, cellophane treat bags, flavoring extracts, food coloring, and chocolate in bulk.

www.candylandcrafts.com
www.fancyflours.com
www.joanns.com
www.kingarthurflour.com
www.kitchenkrafts.com
www.michaels.com
www.streichs.com
www.sugarcraft.com
www.surlatable.com
www.williamssonoma.com
www.wilton.com

Index

Numbers in **bold** (for example, **33**) are photograph numbers, and can be used to locate candies in the photograph section. All other numbers are page numbers.

Acknowledgments

A big thank you to Quirk Books for the opportunity to work with them again. I'm grateful for their support of my creative endeavors. Huge thanks to my recipe testers: Robyn Beechuk, Renee Ting, Patricia Lee, Jennifer Kimura, and Sarah Wong. Without their generosity and talent, the candies in this book wouldn't be nearly as delicious!

Additional thanks to: Jane Dimmel for generously sharing her family recipe for peanut brittle—I'm also dedicating this book to her husband Drew, who is the biggest candy lover I know; Margaret McGuire, my editor, for her unending support and her skillful editing that shaped this book into its delicious final form; Tucker + Hossler for an inspired photo shoot—their skill and artistry is a joy to watch; all the readers of my Web site Dessert First—their enthusiasm and friendship kept me going while writing this book; my parents and sisters for their continued love, and for understanding when I disappeared into my kitchen for weeks at a time.

And to Mike, for all his patience and love, for stepping up as a recipe tester when I was overwhelmed, for putting up with caramel and chocolate all over the house, for making me laugh, and for keeping me sane throughout the whole crazy process. You're the best, and I love you.

More Quirk Field Guides

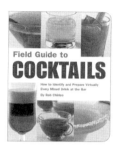

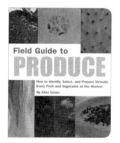

**Available at www.quirkbooks.com
and Wherever Books Are Sold**

irreference \ir-'ef-(ə-)rən(t)s\ *n* (2009)

   1 : irreverent reference
   2 : real information that also entertains or amuses

How-Tos. Quizzes. Instructions.
Recipes. Crafts. Jokes.
Trivia. Games. Tricks.
Quotes. Advice. Tips.

Learn something. Or not.

VISIT IRREFERENCE.COM
The New Quirk Books Web Site